YCP

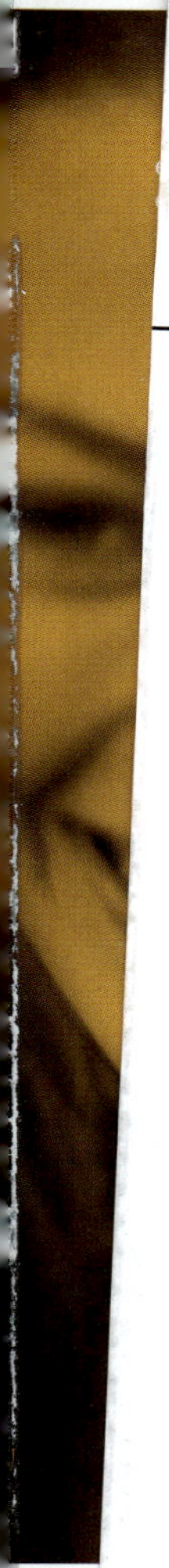

The Citizenship Foundation would like to thank Hodder Education for their support in the production of this fourteenth edition.

Law Society Charity
The Law Society
Solicitors Making a Difference

We would also like to thank the **Law Society Charity** for their continued support for this and other projects.

Editor and main author Tony Thorpe

Concept devised by Andrew Phillips OBE, President of the Citizenship Foundation.

This edition has been prepared by Ruth Cohen, Richard Siddall and Tony Thorpe. We are also very grateful to Lisa Hallgarten, Dan Mace, Lord Northbourne, and lawyers from Allen & Overy, Clifford Chance, DLA Piper, Foot Anstey, Kennedys, Linklaters, Olswang, Slaughter and May, and White & Case for their help in updating and correcting the text.

We would also like to thank Matrix Chambers for their support.

Designed and illustrated by Nomad Graphique, Mike Gibas, Lena Whitaker, Laura Emms, Mark Askam and Adam Williams.

Photographs AbleStock, iStockphoto, PhotoDisc, PhotoAlto, Nomad Graphique, Ingram Publishing, Metropolitan Police Service.

British Library Cataloguing in Publication Data
A catalogue record for this title is available from the British Library
ISBN: 978 0340 990 476
First published 1994
Fourteenth Edition 2009

Impression number 5 4 3 2 1
Year 2012 2011 2010 2009

Printed in Dubai for Hodder Education, an Hachette UK Company, 338 Euston Road, London NW1 3BH.

young citizen's passport

life

INDIVIDUALS ENGAGING IN SOCIETY

Citizenship Foundation

sex

Not the whole story

Although sex is discussed much more now than it was in the past, most people at some stage in their lives get confused about what they should and should not be doing. Probably the best advice is:

- **don't believe everything you hear;**
- **decide what feels right for you;**
- **talk to your partner and think about their point of view.**

You don't have to do anything that you are not comfortable with. Nor should you expect your partner to. There is no golden age by which you should have had sex. Some people will choose not to because they are not interested, or because there hasn't yet been the right opportunity, or because they want to wait until they are married. There's plenty of time and it's OK to opt out.

Pressurising someone into going further than they want, as well as being morally wrong, can reach a stage where it is also against the law. For example, even kissing or touching someone without their agreement can be an assault. In law, both people must agree to what they are doing (known as consent), and they must understand what is happening. The person who gets someone drunk in order to go to bed with them, or takes advantage of their drunken state, risks being charged with rape. (See **safety**, page 23.)

Age of consent

Under the *Sexual Offences Act 2003*, both boys and girls must be 16 years of age before they can legally agree to have sex.

Unlawful sex

A person who is under 18 years of age who has sex with someone under 16 can be prosecuted and sent to prison for up to five years. These measures are designed to protect children and teenagers from abuse. However the law has not been drawn up with the intention of criminalising sexual activity where both partners agree and no harm results. In these cases, prosecution is unlikely.

An adult, aged 18 or over, who takes part in sexual activity with someone aged 13–15 (even if they agree) commits an offence and can be imprisoned for up to 14 years; however such adults may be found not guilty if they can show that it was reasonable to believe that their partner was 16 or over.

An adult who has sex with a child of 12 or under can be imprisoned for life, and cannot say in their defence that they believed the child was 16 or over.

Grooming

It is an offence, under the *Sexual Offences Act 2003*, for an adult to set out to meet someone under 16 with the intention of sexually abusing them – either then, or later.

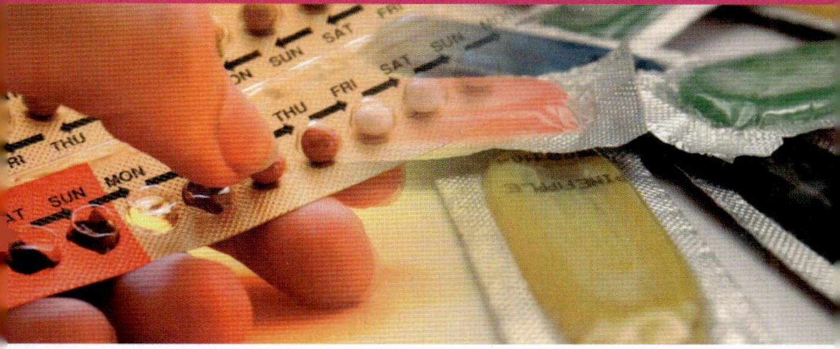

Lesbian and gay sex

For women

Lesbian relationships are lawful. The law says nothing about lesbian relationships specifically.

For men Gay relationships are lawful if both men consent and are 16 or over.

For all There are still difficulties for lesbian and gay people in a society where some people and faiths don't fully recognise a person's right to a gay relationship.

If you need to talk to someone who understands, see **contacts** for groups who may be able to help.

Contraception

Each person who has sex is responsible for guarding against the risks to both people. It is important to know how to use contraceptives properly and how they affect your body. Good advice is therefore vital. For this you can go to a family planning clinic, your doctor, or a Brook Advisory Centre. If you're under 16, a doctor can prescribe contraceptives for you without telling your parents – as long as the doctor believes that you are mature enough to understand what is being proposed and that there is no risk to your health or safety. Condoms can easily be bought from supermarkets, garages, chemists, from slot machines in toilets and by mail order. Femidoms, which are a form of sheath for women, are sold in chemists. These, and condoms, are available free from family planning clinics.

The British Pregnancy Advisory Service now prescribes emergency contraception in advance of need, see **contacts**.

Emergency

If you have had sex without using contraception – or used a condom that split – emergency contraception is available to stop you becoming pregnant.

This form of contraception is for emergencies only. It is not as reliable as the Pill or a condom, and does not protect against sexual diseases. Some people also believe it represents a form of early abortion.

The emergency contraceptive pill is available free from your GP or a family planning clinic, and should be taken within 72 hours of unprotected sex. It can also be bought from most chemists – but some do not sell it to girls under 16.

An IUD, which may also be used to prevent a pregnancy must be fitted by a trained doctor.

pregnancy

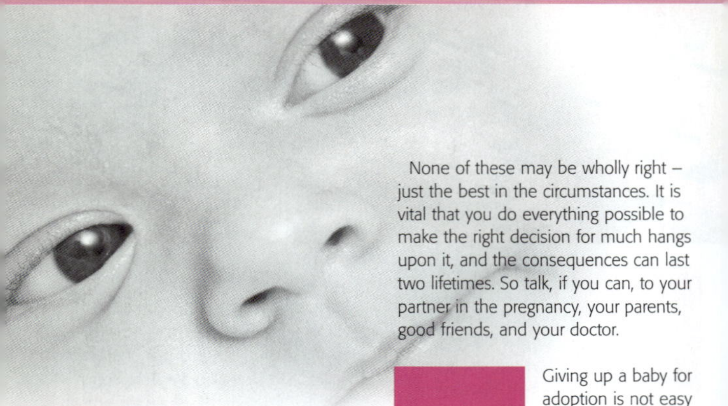

You think you're pregnant

Your period is late and you think you might be pregnant. What do you do? To find out if you are expecting a baby, you can…

- **see your doctor;**
- **buy a pregnancy testing kit from a chemist or supermarket pharmacy. These are generally accurate and cost between £6–£10;**
- **visit a family planning clinic or a Brook Advisory Centre, who will give a free test with an immediate result.**

If you talk to a doctor or nurse, they must keep the conversation confidential, unless they think you have been harmed or abused and that telling someone else is essential to prevent further harm.

What if it's positive?

You will have three choices: to go through with the pregnancy and bring up your child; to give the baby over to be adopted; or to have an abortion and terminate the pregnancy.

None of these may be wholly right – just the best in the circumstances. It is vital that you do everything possible to make the right decision for much hangs upon it, and the consequences can last two lifetimes. So talk, if you can, to your partner in the pregnancy, your parents, good friends, and your doctor.

Adoption

Giving up a baby for adoption is not easy – for the mother or father. It's best to talk to someone about this, such as your doctor or someone at the antenatal clinic, as soon as possible.

The adoption will probably be handled by a social worker who will discuss the kind of family the birth parents want their child to grow up in, and will try to find out as much as possible about the birth family to pass on to the adopters. Adopters can be single or married, and the law also allows unmarried and same sex couples to apply for joint adoption.

When the child has settled down with the new family, the adoptive parents can apply to the adoption centre at the local county court for an adoption order, which will be granted if the court is satisfied that all is well.

Neither birth parent has the right to see their child after she or he has been adopted, although sometimes the court can give permission for contact. Once they are 18, a child may seek to get in touch with their birth parents. Help and advice for anyone affected by adoption is available through the British Association for Adoption and Fostering, see **contacts**.

likely to suffer excessive emotional strain.

Ninety per cent of abortions in Britain take place within the first 13 weeks of pregnancy, although abortion is legal up to 24 weeks and, after that, only in exceptional circumstances.

The procedure that the doctor will follow will be largely determined by the stage of the woman's pregnancy. What is known as medical abortion, involving two clinic visits and two doses of medication, is normally performed within the first nine weeks. An aspiration abortion, in which the contents of the uterus are drawn out, is undertaken using a local anaesthetic. In these circumstances doctors insist that a capable person accompanies the patient to and from the hospital or clinic.

A young woman under 16 may be referred for abortion without her parent's consent if doctors agree that she is mature enough to understand the procedure involved. However, the doctor will also advise and help the young woman to think about talking to their parent or carer, who will be able to provide valuable support, once they have overcome any initial shock or concern.

The earlier in pregnancy an abortion takes place, the safer it is. It is also easier to arrange and more likely that it can be provided locally. Most areas can provide abortion up to twelve weeks; after this, it may be necessary to travel to a larger town or city.

The father, whether he is married to the mother or not, has no right to force or prevent the mother from having an abortion.

A doctor does not have to carry out an abortion if it is against his or her conscience. If this happens, you can arrange to see another doctor.

Abortion

A decision by a woman to have an abortion involves practical considerations about how having a child is likely to affect her future, her current relationships and her responsibilities. It may also involve questions of feelings and values. Some people have strong objections to abortion, based on their personal beliefs, family, culture, or religion.

For anyone thinking of having an abortion it is almost always helpful to talk to someone about it. This can be a doctor, staff at a family planning clinic, or someone from one of the other organisations listed in **contacts**.

The law

Abortion in England and Wales is controlled by the *Abortion Act 1967*. This states that an abortion may be legally carried out if two doctors agree that:

- **continuing the pregnancy would risk the life of, or cause serious permanent injury to the mother; or**
- **the mother is less than 24 weeks pregnant and continuation would risk injury to her physical or mental health or that of her other children; or**
- **there is a substantial risk that the child will be born severely handicapped.**

Concern over the mother's mental health is a common reason for doctors to allow an abortion – particularly if they feel she is

hiv and aids

What is HIV?

To understand HIV – standing for human immunodeficiency virus – you have to know something about the immune system that stops us from getting ill.

Blood plays an important part in our body's defence against illness. It contains millions of cells, about one per cent of which are white cells. A particularly important type of white cell is called the t-helper cell, and one of the jobs of these cells is to fight off infection.

HIV is a virus that attacks the t-helper cells. If it grows inside these cells, and other germs get into our body, we have no way of fighting infection. We become ill and develop what is called acquired immune deficiency syndrome, known as AIDS.

HIV is the cause of AIDS, although not everyone who is HIV positive goes on to suffer the effects associated with the syndrome.

How do you get HIV?

The HIV virus is found in the blood, semen, or vaginal fluid of a person with HIV or AIDS. Infection takes place when these fluids pass from an infected person into the bloodstream of someone else. This can happen in several ways:

- **by having unprotected sex with someone who already has the HIV virus. This means putting a penis into a vagina or anus without using a condom. The risk of contracting HIV infection through unprotected oral sex is thought to be much lower – but transmission is possible if semen, vaginal fluid, or menstrual blood come into contact with bleeding gums or mouth infections. You can help to protect yourself from HIV infection through sex by using a condom;**
- **by sharing or using a hypodermic needle, that has already been used by someone with HIV, leading to the exchange of a small amount of infected blood;**
- **as a result of a mother with HIV passing it on to her baby whilst it is growing inside her.**

Blood transfusions in industrialised countries should be safe as the blood used is routinely screened.

Anyone who feels they may be at risk of HIV or AIDS should seek medical advice and help, see **contacts**.

How don't you get HIV?

The HIV virus dies quickly once outside the body. Because of this, you don't get HIV from:

• hugging • kissing, including French kisses • sharing towels or cutlery • swimming • toilet seats • sharing musical instruments • giving blood.

HIV and the law

It is a serious offence for a person who knows they are HIV positive to have unprotected sex with a partner, without telling them that they are infected. If the partner contracts HIV as a result, the carrier may be charged with causing grievous bodily harm and, if found guilty, face a term of imprisonment.

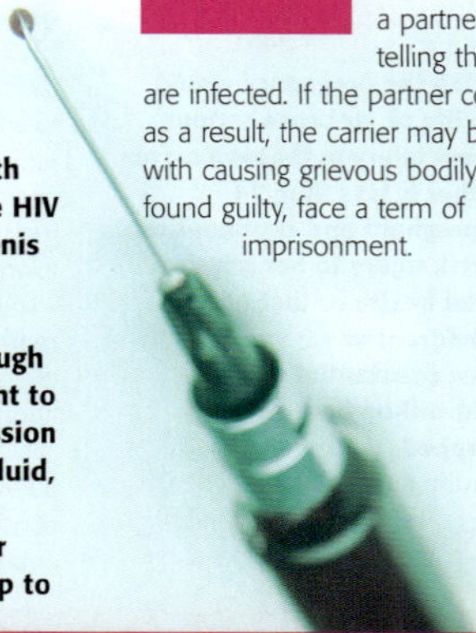

SEXUALLY TRANSMITTED INFECTIONS (STIs)

There are a number of sexually transmitted infections (such as chlamydia, gonorrhoea, hepatitis and syphilis) that are caught from sexual contact with people who have the infection themselves. Some infections cause sores and pains in or around the area of your sexual organ, but others can affect different parts of the body. Hepatitis, for example, causes an inflammation of the liver and may be transmitted by unprotected penetrative or oral sex.

If you have any concerns, see a doctor straightaway, and don't have sex with anyone until the condition has cleared up, otherwise you put your partner's health at risk as well. Seeking urgent treatment for STIs could save you from suffering from permanent health problems in the future.

However, not all STIs show signs of infection. Anyone who has sex with someone who is not their regular partner is particularly at risk, especially if they fail to use a condom. Chlamydia, for example, can pass undetected for some time, but may eventually produce pain and discomfort, and cause infertility in men and give women problems in conceiving.

Advice and treatment on sexually transmitted infections is available from clinics dealing with family planning, pregnancy or genito-urinary medicine, as well as family doctors. It is entirely confidential, although if you are under 16, the doctor may be reluctant to do anything without consulting your parents. If this is the case, it is worth checking first.

HIV and work

If you have HIV or AIDS, you are under no legal obligation to tell your employer. However, there is also no law stopping your employer from asking questions about whether you are infected with HIV. For example, employers may, if they wish, ask all those who apply for a job if they are HIV positive, or to take an HIV test. However, if they do, this information must not be used to discriminate against anyone.

The government advises health care workers who believe themselves to be at risk from infection to seek medical advice immediately. Your employer has a legal duty to treat the information that you are HIV positive as confidential. As a rule, employers are not entitled to tell other workers that an employee is infected with HIV, without his or her permission.

Since December 2005, it has been against the law, under the Disability Discrimination Act, for employers to discriminate against someone with HIV/AIDS.

If you are worried about HIV or AIDS, see **contacts** for support and help.

Prostitution

Prostitutes sell sex for money. They can be either men or women. It is an offence for a prostitute to attract "business" in public (called soliciting) and for someone to try to obtain the services of a prostitute from a motor vehicle that they are in, or have just got out of. Under the *Sexual Offences Act 2003*, it is an offence for a person to pay for sex with someone under 18.

If the police become aware that a young person under the age of 18 is involved in prostitution, they will almost certainly inform social services who will decide whether to apply for an order to take that person into care.

drugs and the law

Controlled drugs

All drugs produce some kind of change in the way a person's body or mind works, and the availability of most drugs – whether aspirins, alcohol or amphetamines – is controlled by law.

The main law covering the use of dangerous drugs in the UK is the *Misuse of Drugs Act 1971*. Under this Act, drugs that people might misuse have been placed on a list of controlled drugs, and it is an offence to possess, produce or supply anyone with them. The list of controlled drugs is divided into three categories – Classes A, B and C.

CLASS A DRUGS

Cocaine is a white powder that is injected, rubbed onto gums, or snorted through a tube. Crack is cocaine treated with chemicals, so it can be smoked. Both give a high, followed by a rapid down. The only way to maintain the high is to keep taking the drug – but regular use leads to sickness, sleeplessness, weight loss, and addiction.

Heroin is made from the opium poppy and can be smoked, sniffed or injected. It comes as a white powder when pure. Street heroin is usually brownish white. Heroin slows down the brain and, at first, gives a feeling of total relaxation. Repeated use creates dependency. Overdosing causes unconsciousness and often death – particularly if used

CLASS B DRUGS

Amphetamines, sold as pills or powder, were developed to treat depression. They give a feeling of energy and confidence, but increasing doses are needed to keep up the effect. The downside is anxiety, insomnia, irritability and less resistance to disease and, as with all illegal drugs, there is no guarantee that they do not contain other harmful substances.

Barbiturates are used in medicine to help people who cannot sleep. They produce feelings of drowsiness and relief from anxiety. They are sold as a powder or coloured capsule. Regular use creates dependency. They are extremely dangerous when taken with alcohol or other drugs.

Cannabis was reclassified to a Class B drug in January 2009. Possession of cannabis is an offence, with a maximum sentence of two years' imprisonment and an unlimited fine. A sentence of up to 14 years and an unlimited fine may be given for dealing in and supplying cannabis.

People over 18 found possessing cannabis are likely to receive a warning and have the drug confiscated, but could be arrested if smoking in public. Repeat offenders face arrest and prosecution.

Someone under 18 caught with cannabis is likely to be arrested and taken to a police station, and given a warning or reprimand. If it's not their first offence they will be given a final warning or will be charged. If they receive a warning they will be referred to the local youth offending team.

The effects of cannabis vary from one person to another. Some feel relaxed and happy, but the downside can be moodiness, anxiety, and difficulties with memory. Heavy users risk great tiredness, mental health problems, and cancer – from the chemical constituents.

with other drugs, such as alcohol.

LSD, also known as acid, is a man-made substance, sold impregnated on blotting paper (often printed with cartoon characters or in colourful patterns) and dissolved on the tongue. It usually takes about an hour to work, and lasts up to 12 hours. The effects depend on the strength of the dose and the user's mood. It generally distorts feelings, vision and hearing, and bad trips lead to depression and panic, or worse, if the user is already anxious.

Ecstasy, or E, is usually sold as tablets of different shapes and colour. It makes the user feel friendly and full of energy, and sound and colours can seem much more intense. However, the comedown can leave the user tired and low – often for days. Regular users can have problems sleeping, and some women find it makes their periods heavier. Ecstasy affects the body's temperature control and it may cause the user to overheat and dehydrate. There is no guarantee that tablets sold as ecstasy do not contain some other ingredients. This can make their use unpredictable and dangerous.

Magic mushrooms grow in the wild and contain hallucinogenic chemicals that, when eaten, have similar effects to LSD. It is an offence to possess, sell or supply magic mushrooms in all forms.

CLASS C DRUGS

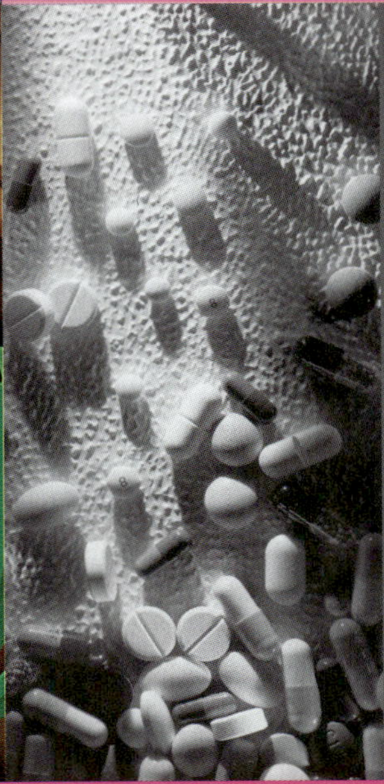

Tranquillisers cause lower alertness, and affect people who drive or operate machinery. A number of anabolic steroids are also on the list of controlled drugs after concern over their misuse in sport and bodybuilding.

drugs and the law

The risks

- There is no way of knowing exactly what is in drugs made or obtained illegally. This makes them unpredictable and dangerous.
- All drugs have side effects that may be dangerous and even fatal – particularly if they are mixed or taken regularly.
- Anyone using shared needles, filters or spoons, risks becoming infected with hepatitis or HIV, the virus that leads to AIDS.
- Hepatitis C is a newly discovered virus that can cause severe long-term liver damage. It is caused by blood-to-blood contact, generally through sharing needles when injecting drugs.
- Employers and head teachers have a legal duty to confiscate drugs found at work or school and hand them to the police as quickly as possible.
- Illegal drug-taking places a person's job, school, or college place at risk.
- A person prosecuted for illegal drug use will not necessarily be sent to prison, but could end up with a criminal record. However, a prison sentence is a strong possibility for someone found guilty of supply.

Possession

Possession of a controlled drug is an offence, even if it's only a tiny amount. First-time offenders in possession of Class C drugs are likely to receive a reprimand or warning. Repeat offenders and users who smoke cannabis in public may be taken to court.

Supply

It is an offence under the *Misuse of Drugs Act 1971* to supply or to offer to supply someone with a controlled drug. Obviously this includes the sale of drugs – but it is still an offence even if money does not change hands. Giving a controlled drug to a friend, or sharing a drug at a party by passing it from one person to another, is still seen in law as supply. (See **leisure**, page 94.)

It is also an offence if the substance sold is not actually a controlled drug, but the seller claimed or believed it to be one.

Production

It is an offence under the *Misuse of Drugs Act 1971* to produce any controlled drug. This includes letting someone use your kitchen or a room for this purpose.

Growing cannabis comes under this

BRIEF CASE: Dennis

Dennis bought 1,000 tabs of what he thought was LSD, and was caught by the police trying to sell them. When the tablets were analysed they were found not to contain LSD, but a harmless vegetable product that was not at all illegal. Despite this, Dennis was accused and found guilty of supplying an illegal or controlled drug, because his intention was to supply LSD.

heading, and is an offence if you knew what you were doing.

Police powers

If a police officer has reasonable grounds to suspect that someone is in possession of a controlled drug, the officer can search that person and their vehicle and seize anything that seems to be evidence of an offence.

Glue sniffing

The effect of solvent abuse is rather like getting drunk on alcohol. However, it takes effect more quickly as the substances enter the bloodstream through the lungs rather than the stomach. Sniffers may experience hallucinations and, if plastic bags are used, may become unconscious or choke on their own vomit. Glue sniffing itself is not against the law, but it is an offence, under the *Intoxicating Substances (Supply) Act 1985* to supply a solvent such as glue, lighter fuel or other substances to a young person under 18, if there is reasonable cause to believe that the fumes might be inhaled.

Tobacco and alcohol

In October 2007, the minimum legal age for buying tobacco in England and Wales rose from 16 to 18 years. Shopkeepers who sell tobacco or cigarettes to anyone who seems to be under the age of 18 may face heavy fines.

Smoking is now banned in virtually all enclosed public places throughout the UK. These include shops, offices, factories, pubs and bars.

Alcohol may generally not be sold to anyone below the age of 18. For more details, see **leisure**, pages 88–89.

Information

The National Drugs Helpline is open 24 hours a day, every day of the year, tel (free) 0800 77 66 00 or email frank@talktofrank.com

BRIEF CASE: Alex

Alex was one of a group who bought and sold drugs for themselves and other students at their university. One day, his friend Paul took an overdose of heroin and died. It was Alex who had supplied the drug. A court sentenced him to five years in prison.

Doctors

Confidentiality

Once you're 16, you can decide about your own health care – although, strictly speaking, doctors don't need to consult parents of a patient who is under 16, as long as they believe the patient fully understands what is being proposed. Patients also have a right of confidentiality. Nothing they say to their doctor should be passed on to anyone else – not even the fact that they made an appointment. However, in special cases, information might be shared if the safety of the patient or someone else is judged to be at risk, or if there is a legal requirement to do so.

General practitioners

Everyone living in the UK, including visitors from overseas, is entitled to register with a GP. A list of local doctors is available from your local Health Authority, main post office, library, tourist information office, and Citizens Advice Bureau.

You have the right to change your GP at any time. You don't have to explain your reasons for doing so or tell the doctor concerned. However, a GP does not have to accept you as a patient either, as long as they have reasonable grounds for refusal which must be given to you in writing. If you are refused in this way, your local Primary Care Trust or Health Board must give you details of local GPs. New patients are entitled to a health examination when they join a practice.

If you are staying for up to three months in another part of the United Kingdom, you can ask to be registered with another GP on a temporary basis. But if you are leaving home and going to college or university it's probably better to register with a new doctor in the town or city where you are staying, so you are guaranteed all the services of the practice if you ever need them. It's helpful to provide your medical card or National Health number when you register.

PRESCRIPTIONS

There are now no prescription charges in Wales. Prescriptions in England are free if you:

- **are under 16 or 16-18 and in full-time education; or**
- **are pregnant or have had a baby in the last twelve months and have a valid exemption certificate; or**
- **suffer from a serious illness;**
- **you or your partner receive Income Support, income-based Jobseeker's Allowance, Income-related Employment and Support Allowance or have an NHS Tax Credit Exemption Certificate; or**
- **your name is on a current HC2 charges certificate.**

Further details are available from GPs, the Citizens Advice Bureau and from libraries.

Anyone in England claiming a free prescription may be asked to provide proof that they are entitled to do so. A person who cannot do this should not be refused the prescription, but a check on their entitlement may be made by a prescription fraud team.

If you don't have these, you will need to know your place of birth and the name and address of the doctor or practice with which you were previously registered.

Records Under the *Data Protection Act 1998*, you have a general right to see all your medical records – whether they are held on paper or on computer. You are also entitled to ask for a copy to take away. Access, however, may be refused if the doctor believes that seeing your records may cause you or someone else serious physical or mental harm.

Your GP or the hospital may ask you to pay for this service. The maximum charge to see your records (either on paper or on screen) is £10. The maximum charge for a copy of a computer held record is also £10 – and £50 if any records are held manually.

If you believe that the information on your records is not correct, you may ask for it to be changed. The doctor does not have to agree, but is required to note on your records what you have said.

health

DENTISTS

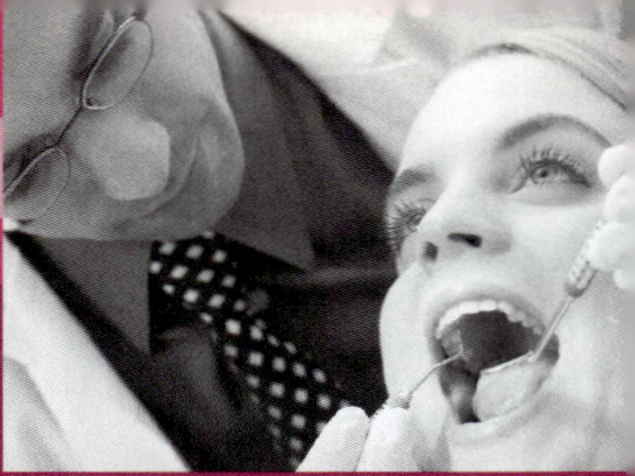

All British citizens are entitled to dental treatment provided by the National Health Service. However – unlike medical treatment from a GP – dental treatment is not always available free of charge.

NHS patients pay £16.50 for a check-up, £45.60 for treatment such as fillings or extractions, and up to a maximum of £198 (April 2008) for more complex work.

Dental treatment is free if:

- **you are under 18 (under 25 in Wales – dental examination only), or under 19 and still in full-time education; or**
- **you are pregnant or have had a baby in the twelve months before treatment starts; or**
- **your name is on a current HC2 charges certificate; or**
- **you or your partner receive Income Support, income-based Jobseeker's Allowance, Income-related Employment and Support Allowance or have an NHS Tax Credit Exemption Certificate.**

An NHS dentist cannot charge a patient who fails to keep an appointment or makes a last minute cancellation, but the dentist can remove the patient from their list.

Not all dentists provide NHS treatment. To find a list of NHS dentists in your area, look on the NHS website, www.nhs.uk, call NHS Direct (see contacts), or look in the Yellow Pages, under 'dental surgeons'. You don't have to be registered with a dentist to get NHS treatment; you can contact any surgery providing NHS treatment and ask if they have any NHS appointments available. However, it is usually much easier to obtain treatment if you have regular appointments with the same dentist.

Before each course of treatment, you will receive a treatment plan, showing the work the dentist intends to carry out and what it will cost. The dentist may offer to treat you privately, but should not place pressure on you by implying that the treatment is not available on the NHS. You do not have to accept the treatment being offered.

If you need emergency treatment and are not registered with a dentist, contact a local NHS dentist to see if they can take you on an emergency basis, or get in touch with your local Primary Care Trust (PCT) in England, or Health Board in Wales. Many areas have dental access centres, providing NHS treatment and advice for emergency work and for those not registered for regular treatment. Details are available from your PCT.

Opticians Eye tests are no longer free to everyone. You will get a free test if you:

- **are under 16 or under 19 and in full-time education; or**
- **are blind partially sighted or need complex lenses; or**
- **are diagnosed with diabetes, or glaucoma; or**
- **you or your partner receive Income Support, income-based Jobseeker's Allowance, or have an NHS Tax Credit Exemption Certificate; or**
- **your name is on a current HC2 charges certificate.**

If you need glasses, you may be entitled to help with buying them, particularly if you are unemployed or a student on a low income. Further information is available from opticians, the Citizens Advice Bureau and booklet HC11, *Help with health costs*, available from libraries.

Complaints If you have a complaint about the NHS or your treatment, it's important to make it as soon as possible. Advice is available from NHS Direct, tel 0845 46 47.

Tattoos It's illegal for a person to be given a tattoo if they are under 18.

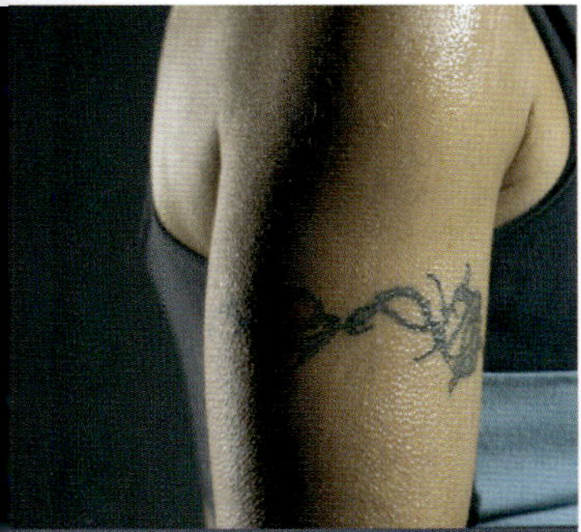

NHS DIRECT

NHS Direct is a 24-hour help and information service providing confidential information on particular health conditions and what to do if you are feeling ill, tel 0845 46 47. You may ask for an interpreter to provide advice in your own language.

NHS Direct Online is a website providing information about health services and a variety of medical conditions and treatments, www.nhsdirect.nhs.uk.

NHS Walk-In Centres in England provide treatment for minor injuries and illnesses seven days a week. You don't need an appointment and will be seen by an experienced NHS nurse. There are Centres in many towns and cities. For more details contact NHS Direct or visit the National Health Service website, www.nhs.uk, and go to 'Find services' then 'Walk-in centres'.

The right to die The law states that a doctor may give a patient a painkilling drug, which shortens their life, as long as the intention is to relieve pain and suffering and not to kill. If the drug is given with the intention of ending that person's life, the doctor can face a charge of murder.

It is possible to make what is called a living will (known in law as an advance directive) setting out how you would like to be treated if you ever lose the capacity to make or convey a decision. You must clearly understand what you are doing when you give the directive and, if it is done properly, it is legally binding on the doctor. But an advance directive cannot authorise a doctor to do anything unlawful.

Wills Anyone aged 18 or over can make a will, provided they are capable of understanding what they are doing. There is no lower age limit for people in the forces on active service, or sailors at sea.

Blood There's no legal minimum age to become a blood donor, but the National Blood Service won't accept anyone under 17. Donors usually give about three quarters of a pint up to three times a year.

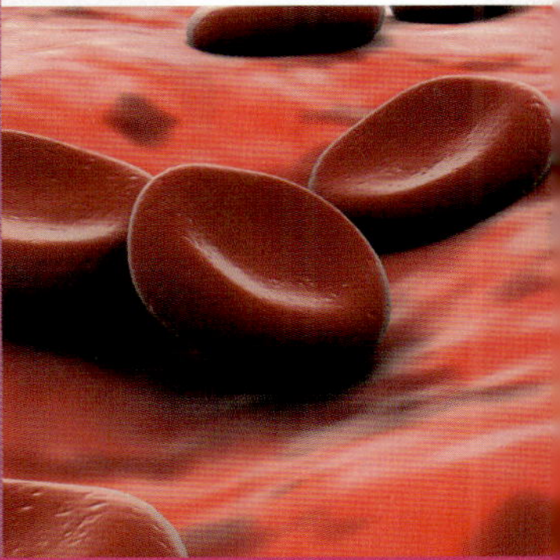

Mental health

Most people who receive hospital treatment for a mental illness are there either because they choose to be, or because they have taken the advice of a doctor or social worker.

They are known in law as *informal patients*. In a relatively small number of cases, a person who refuses to be examined or treated will be admitted to hospital compulsorily under the *Mental Health Act 1983*. This will be done either in the interests of their own safety or for the protection of others. This is often called *sectioning*.

An application for compulsory detention is normally made by a social worker, supported (except in an emergency) in writing by two doctors. One of the doctors should be known to the patient personally, and the other must have experience in the treatment of mental illness. The patient's nearest relative must also be consulted. An application for compulsory detention can also be made by the patient's nearest relative.

Emergency

In an emergency, a person can be admitted to hospital for up to 72 hours on the application of a relative or social worker, supported by a doctor.

Emergency powers are also available to the police, who can remove someone from a public place who appears to be mentally ill and in need of care. This person would normally be taken to a place of safety, such as a hospital for up to 72 hours.

Leaving hospital

Informal patients can leave hospital whenever they wish, unless the doctor feels that this would be a mistake and applies for a detention order. The procedure for the releasing of patients detained compulsorily is more complex. More information is available from NHS Direct or MIND, the mental health charity. See **contacts** for details.

young citizen's passport

safety

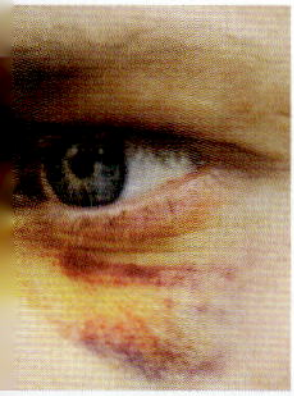

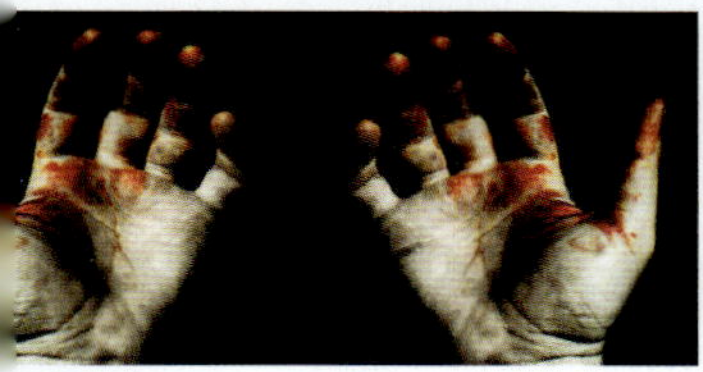

INDIVIDUALS ENGAGING IN SOCIETY

Citizenship Foundation

Fighting Back

If you're threatened or hit, it's usually better to try to avoid a fight by talking to your attacker or backing off calmly.

If you can't do this, the law says that you can use reasonable force to defend yourself, someone else, or property. This means that you're entitled to fight back, but not to go over the top and beat up the other person. If you do, you will have also committed an offence.

There is no law which says that you must report a crime to the police, but if you want to claim compensation for your injuries, the crime must first have been reported to the police.

Arrest – doing it yourself

If there isn't a police officer present and you see someone committing a serious offence, or have reasonable grounds for believing that they have committed one, you can make a citizen's arrest. But, take care. People have been hurt and even killed trying to do their civic duty. The best advice is to take in as much as you can about the incident, and then to ring the police. If you do get involved, remember that an ordinary person only has the power to make an arrest for a serious offence – such as theft, serious assault, or burglary. Don't arrest someone for parking on a double yellow line.

Neighbourhood patrols also come up against this problem. They can't arrest someone who they think is about to commit an offence (it must already have been done), nor can they use excessive force – otherwise they can face charges of assault and wrongful arrest.

Victims of violent crime

Victims of violent crime can apply to the Criminal Injuries Compensation Authority for compensation for their injuries – which must be serious enough to receive an award. The crime must be reported to the police as soon as possible, and an application for compensation made within two years of the incident that caused the injury. However, all cases are treated individually and an exception can be made if, for example, the delay in reporting was caused by the after effects of the crime.

Victim Support runs a helpline and gives advice to victims of crime. Their number is in the local phone book, see **contacts**.

If you are a victim of crime and called as a witness, you can arrange to visit a courtroom before the case starts, reserve a seat for someone accompanying you, wait separately from other people, or talk to somebody from Victim Support. Details are given in the Victim's Charter and the Courts' Charter, see **contacts**.

BRIEF CASE: Raj

Raj ran an off-licence, and had twice been the victim of armed robbery. One night, a man carrying a long knife came into the shop demanding money from the till. As Raj was being held with a knife to his throat, his brother came through from the back and the robber ran off. Raj was so angry that he got into his van and chased the man down the street knocking him down and killing him. Raj was found guilty of manslaughter and sentenced to two and a half years' imprisonment. The Court decided that he could not have been acting in self-defence because he was, by that time, not being attacked or threatened.

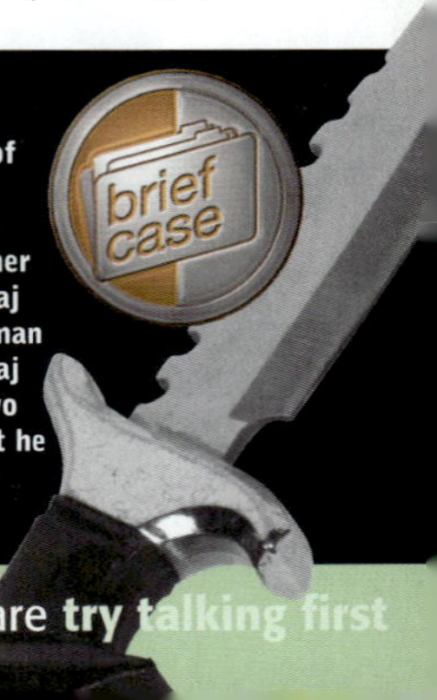

Self defence If you carry something to use for self-defence, you run the risk of actually breaking the law yourself. Under the *Prevention of Crime Act 1953*, it is an offence to carry something made, adapted, or intended to cause injury to someone. This includes things like a knife, bicycle chain, or a sharpened comb. The penalty is a prison sentence, or a fine, or both.

Knives Under the *Criminal Justice Act 1988* and the *Offensive Weapons Act 1996*, it is an offence to have anything with a blade or sharp point in a public place. Folded pocket knives are allowed as long as the blade is less than 3″ long and not used in a threatening way. Schools are specifically mentioned as places where articles with blades or points must not be carried, and the police have the power to enter and search school premises if they have a good reason to believe that an offence of this kind has been committed. The penalty is a prison sentence, a fine, or both.

SOME WORDS THEY USE

Assault & battery The word 'assault' is not used in law in quite the same way as in everyday speech. Strictly speaking, an assault takes place when someone causes a person to fear that they are about to suffer immediate unlawful physical violence. If this fear becomes reality and force is actually used against someone without their consent, the assault becomes a battery, however slight the force. Normally assault and battery take place at the same time. But it is possible to be assaulted without battery (raising an arm and shouting threats without hitting anyone), and to be battered without assault (hitting someone from behind without warning).

Burglary Burglary takes place when a person enters a building without permission, intending to steal, cause unlawful damage, or seriously harm someone. Even if nothing is taken or done, a crime has still been committed. It's enough in law to prove that the person intended to break the law in this way.

Robbery Stealing something with the use or threat of force.

Theft There are, in law, three parts to theft. A person is guilty of theft who:

- dishonestly takes something, which
- belongs to someone else, and
- intends to deprive that person of it permanently.

harassment

Abusive behaviour Under the *Criminal Justice and Public Order Act 1994*, it is an offence to use threatening, abusive or insulting words or behaviour in public in a way that is likely to cause a person harassment, alarm, or distress. It's also an offence to put up threatening, abusive, or insulting signs or posters. The law is designed to protect anyone who is being treated like this because, for example, of their race, disability, religion or sexuality. Harassment of this kind is a crime – just like any other – and can be reported to the police, who have a duty to investigate and to try to find those responsible. Statements from witnesses will strengthen a case.

Punishment for offences that can be shown to be racially aggravated, such as harassment, assault and criminal damage now carry increased penalties under the *Crime and Disorder Act 1998*.

Local councils also have a number of powers they can use to help tenants or homeowners in their area who are being racially harassed or attacked. They can prosecute residents for harassing or causing nuisance to other residents, they can get a court order stopping people committing certain types of anti-social behaviour, or if those responsible are council tenants, they can evict them from their home.

The police or local authority can also apply for an anti-social behaviour order, see **police and courts**, page 122.

Stalking The *Protection from Harassment Act 1997* became law after a number of cases involving men who were harassing and following women over a long period of time. It is now an offence for someone to behave in a way that they know (or ought to know) amounts to harassment, or puts a person in fear of violence being used against them. For an offence to be

BRIEF CASE: Marcia

Marcia and her 10-year-old son were not the only black people on their estate, but for some reason faced almost continuous trouble from one particular group of boys. Marcia first tried ignoring the problem and then spoke to the boys and tried to talk to their parents. Nothing worked. Eventually she complained to the council who investigated the case and obtained a court order requiring the parents of one of the boys to leave their house, which they rented from the council. The boy's parents appealed, saying it was not their offensive behaviour but that of their son. The appeal was dismissed. The judge said that Marcia and her son should not be deprived of their rights just because the parents could not control their son.

BRIEF CASE: Banned

A Blackburn Rovers' supporter was found guilty of racially aggravated disorderly behaviour, fined £500 and banned from attending football matches in England and Wales for three years. During a match between Blackburn and Birmingham City, the supporter was caught on television cameras making chants and gestures towards City player Dwight Yorke.

committed, the behaviour must take place at least twice and is punishable by imprisonment, a fine and a restraining order. This prohibits the offender from contacting the victim and, for example, going to the area where they live or work.

Someone who feels they might be a victim of harassment can apply to a court for what is known as an injunction, ordering the person committing the offence to keep a certain distance from the victim's house or place of work. The victim can also apply for compensation for the worry they have suffered or for loss of earnings through time off work.

What if it happens to me? It all depends on the situation. If it's an isolated incident and the person is someone you don't know, then it may be best to try and ignore it. If you react and get abusive yourself, you run the risk of finding yourself in a far worse situation.

However, if it's happened before, or you're being harassed where you live, then it's important to tell the police – for your own safety. If you are getting abuse at school, college or at work, try and sort it out with the people concerned, but if that's not possible, or successful, raise it with someone in authority, who will have a legal duty to help you. See also the sections on **discrimination**, pages 46 and 132.

Someone suffering serious abuse or harassment may be able to claim compensation from the Criminal Injuries Compensation Authority, see page 20 and **contacts**.

sexual offences

Sexual assault Under the *Sexual Offences Act 2003*, it is an offence to touch someone intentionally in a sexual way when it is against their wishes and it is clear they have not consented. Sexual assault carries a punishment of up to ten years' imprisonment.

Rape Under the *Sexual Offences Act 2003,* a male aged 10 or over who penetrates somebody's vagina, anus or mouth with his penis, and without their consent, commits the crime of rape. A jury can assume that there was no consent if the victim was asleep, unconscious, disabled or where violence was involved. Rape can be committed against a man or woman. The maximum penalty is life imprisonment. It is also an offence under the same Act to threaten or force a person to have sex against their will, or to give them drugs in the hope that they will give in. It is no defence for a person accused of rape to say that they were drunk and didn't realise what they were doing. Other offences under the *Sexual Offences Act* include spiking someone's drink, flashing, and watching or photographing people without their consent when they are involved in a private act.

If you are raped Although you may not want to tell anyone, most police stations now have women officers who have been trained to deal with victims of sexual offences in a sensitive way. If you are a woman, you can ask to be examined by a female doctor and you can take along your parents or a friend.

sexual offences

The police will be able to gather evidence more easily if you report the rape or assault as soon as possible. Reporting the crime early also makes your evidence more believable in court.

Once a victim tells the police that they have been raped or sexually assaulted, or the suspect has been charged, the victim has the right in law to remain anonymous. The victim cannot be questioned in court by the accused, nor can their name and address or picture be reported in the media. Attempted rape is dealt with in the same way.

Help is available from *Victim Support* and the local *Rape Crisis Centre*, who will talk to any girl or woman who has suffered an unpleasant sexual experience. *Survivors UK* offer an advice service for men, see **contacts**. Victims of rape can apply for compensation to the Criminal Injuries Compensation Authority, although you must have reported the attack to the police to do this, see **contacts**.

Male victims of rape are treated in law in the same way as female victims.

Accused of rape If you are accused of raping someone, immediately contact a solicitor. Rape is a serious crime, and the punishment can be severe.

keeping safe

There are some simple steps that both men and women can take to make themselves safer.

- **If you go out – especially at night – tell someone where you are going. If possible, stay away from known danger spots.**
- **Keep your drink within your sights at all times.**
- **If you're out late, get a lift back if you can with someone you trust, or book a taxi, see page 93.**
- **If you walk home, try to get someone to go with you.**
- **Don't have expensive possessions like mobile phones on show.**
- **Check on the security of your home. Ordinary bolts and chains are not expensive.**
- **Knowing some self-defence can give you a feeling of greater confidence.**
- **If you carry a screech alarm keep it ready in your hand, not in your pocket or handbag.**
- **Men can help by taking care not to frighten women. For example, if you're walking in the same direction as a woman at night, don't walk behind her, cross over the road and walk on the other side.**

Abusive telephone calls It is an offence under the *Communications Act 2003* to make offensive, indecent or malicious phone calls, or to send such texts and emails.

If you get such a call, try not to react and don't start talking to the caller. Don't hang up, but put the receiver down and walk away for a few minutes. Try to do something else, and then put the handset back without checking if the caller is still there. If the phone rings again, pick up the receiver and don't say anything – a genuine caller will speak first. Advice on dealing with calls of this kind is available from BT, tel free 0800 666 700.

young citizen's passport

education

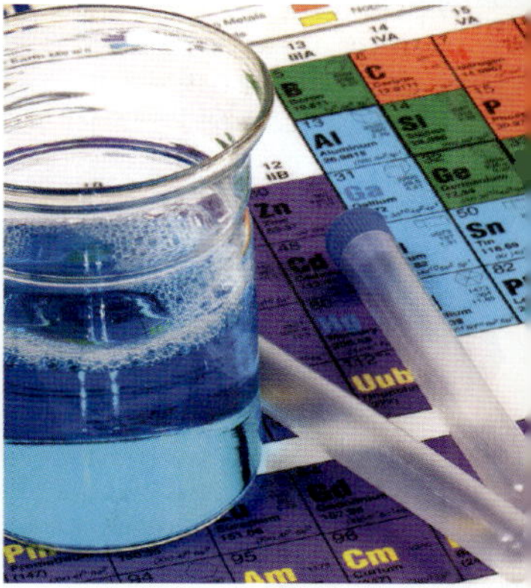

INDIVIDUALS ENGAGING IN SOCIETY

Citizenship Foundation

attendance

Parents have the main responsibility, in law, for their child's education. Under the *Education Act 1996*, it is the duty of parents with children of compulsory school age, to make sure that their child has 'an efficient full-time education suitable to his age, ability and aptitude... by regular attendance at school or otherwise'.

The word 'otherwise' is important here because it allows parents to educate their children out of school. They do not need permission from the local authority, but parents must de-register their child if they are already in school.

Which school?

Under the *Education Act 1996*, parents are able to choose which school they would like their child to attend, and their wishes should be followed wherever possible. However, some schools are very popular and are not able to take all those who apply. Because of this, each school has its own rules for admission, known as criteria, which are used to decide who may or may not be admitted to the school.

If their application is refused, parents can appeal against the decision, but this must be done within a certain time period. Details of how to make the appeal are available from the local authority.

Parents who cannot agree between themselves on a choice of school can ask a court to decide where their child will be educated. In this situation, the court may listen to the wishes of the child concerned.

BRIEF CASE: Peter

After their divorce, Peter's parents couldn't agree about where he should go to school. His mother wanted him to attend a boarding school, his father (with whom Peter lived) said that he couldn't afford the fees and felt Peter should go to a day school. Peter's mother asked a court to decide on her son's future education.

After hearing from both parents, the judge decided that Peter's father could well afford the school fees and so Peter should go to the boarding school. However his father appealed against this, saying that no one in court had asked Peter what he wanted.

The Court of Appeal did just this. Peter, who was 14, told the Court that he wanted to live with his father and couldn't do so if he was at boarding school. The Court of Appeal felt that it was important to take Peter's wishes into account, and said he could go to the school of his choice.

Costs

State education is free and it is against the law for schools to try to make parents pay for books or equipment that pupils need for subjects or activities taken in school hours as part of the National Curriculum. However, charges may be made for:

- **individual music tuition;**
- **materials for practical subjects (if the pupil wants to keep the finished product);**
- **optional trips taken outside school hours;**
- **board and lodging on school trips, even if the activity is part of the school timetable. (Although this does not need to be paid by parents who receive Income Support, income-based Jobseeker's Allowance, or – in certain circumstances – Child Tax Credit.)**

The local education authority has a duty to provide pupils with free school transport or passes if their school is not within 'walking distance' (for children aged eight and over, this is three miles from their home) or where the route home is unsuitable, or it involves crossing a dangerous road. But this does not apply when the child has been offered a place in a suitable school that is closer, which their parents have turned down.

Pupils below the age of 19 are entitled to free school meals if their parents receive Income Support or income-based Jobseeker's Allowance, receive help under the *Immigration and Asylum Act 1999* or (in certain circumstances) Child Tax Credit.

Leaving school or staying on

Under the *Education Act 1996*, pupils must stay on at school until they are 16 and must not leave – even if they are not doing any exams – until the end of the summer term. (Children who are 16 during the summer holidays leave on the same date.) A parent cannot force their child who has passed compulsory school age to stay on at school against their wishes. Under government plans, the school leaving age will rise to 17 in 2013 and to 18 in 2015.

attendance

Truancy

Parents have a legal duty to make sure that their child attends school regularly or is suitably educated elsewhere. If they fail to do this, they may be committing a criminal offence. It is no defence for them to say that they didn't know their child was truanting or that they could do nothing to force them to attend.

To deal with this, the local authority can require a family to work with an educational welfare officer to try to make sure that their child is properly educated. If this fails, or is not realistic, the parents may be prosecuted for a school attendance offence and imprisoned for up to three months, fined up to £2,500, or receive a parenting order. Under the *Crime and Disorder Act 1998*, a police officer who finds a child in a public place may take that child back to school if the officer reasonably believes that the child is of school age and is absent from school without permission.

rules and regulations

Religious worship and education

The *School Standards and Framework Act 1998* requires all pupils in state schools to take part each day in an act of collective worship that should be of a broadly Christian character. Parents can ask for their child to be excused. It is also possible for schools to apply to be allowed to provide non-Christian collective worship.

The law states that all pupils (including those aged between 16 and 18) should receive religious education. Again, parents may withdraw their child from these lessons and make alternative arrangements, but this must not interfere with the attendance of the pupil at school. Pupils cannot opt out of religious education or worship themselves; it must be done by their parents.

Sex education

The law states that all secondary schools must provide sex education for their pupils and in a way that recognises the moral issues involved and the value of family life and stable relationships. However, a parent can ask for their child not to attend sex education lessons and the school must agree, except when they are part of the National Curriculum.

Government guidance states that teachers should deal with the subject of, and questions about, sexuality 'honestly and sensitively' answering appropriate questions and offering support.

Under the *Learning and Skills Act 2000* pupils must learn about the nature of marriage and its importance for family life and bringing up children.

Government guidelines encourage teachers to involve parents and other appropriate professionals if a pupil with a sexual or relationship problem asks them for help.

Punishment

All schools should have a behaviour policy, which students are expected to follow. The policy should be regularly reviewed and outlined to pupils, parents and staff. Punishments must be reasonable (an important word in law). Schools may keep students under 18 in detention outside normal school hours, but parents must be given at least 24 hours' notice of this. Pupils who behave badly on the way to and from school can be disciplined and detentions can take place at weekends during term time and on staff training days – as long as there are satisfactory arrangements for the student's travel.

School uniform

Schools can insist that pupils wear school uniform, as long as it is reasonable and does not discriminate on grounds of sex or race, and pupils can be punished for not wearing the right uniform. Government guidance states that schools should consult students and parents over changes to the uniform, and students should not be excluded for failing to wear the right uniform, unless it is part of a wider pattern of defiant behaviour.

Confiscation

Under the *Education and Inspections Act 2006*, teachers and other authorised members of staff may confiscate – and return at a later date, or dispose of – any item for which in the circumstances it is reasonable to do so. If teachers have acted in a reasonable way, they are not liable for the damage or loss of any item they confiscate.

Illegal drugs or weapons must be seized by teachers and may be handed to the police.

Knives

Schools now have the power to search a pupil whom they suspect may be carrying a dangerous weapon, even without the pupil's or the parent's consent..

CORPORAL PUNISHMENT

Corporal punishment is banned in schools throughout Britain – although a member of staff can use reasonable force to prevent a student from:

- **committing an offence; or**
- **injuring themselves or someone else, or damaging property; or**
- **behaving in a way that threatens the discipline of the school in or out of class.**

However, if a teacher goes beyond what is reasonable, he or she may have committed an assault, which can give rise to both criminal charges and a civil claim for damages.

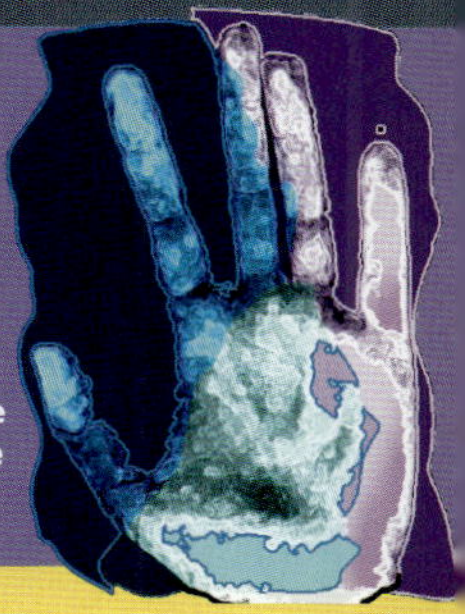

rules and regulations

DRUGS IN SCHOOL

Schools are required to make clear to pupils and parents what action will be taken if pupils are found to be involved in any way with unauthorised drugs within the boundaries of the school. The term 'unauthorised drugs' includes tobacco and alcohol, as well as illegal drugs, and the 'boundaries of the school' may include journeys in school time, work experience, and school trips.

The law School staff may search *school* property such as pupils' lockers or desks if they believe that drugs are stored there. They must seek a pupil's agreement first, but can carry out a search if this is refused. However, staff cannot search pupils' *personal* property, for example a bag, without their consent. If consent is refused, staff may notify pupils' parents or the police.

Schools are encouraged to deal with cases individually and to take into account the circumstances surrounding each incident. Schools are almost always expected to tell parents of their child's involvement with illegal drugs.

School staff may take temporary possession of a substance that they suspect is an illegal drug and must make a full record of every incident involving unauthorised drugs. Schools have no legal obligation to report the matter to the police, although government guidelines recommend that they should do so, and hand over any drugs found for disposal. The decision to inform the police will depend on the nature of the incident and what the school sees as the interests of the pupil and the wider school community. If the police are called, the school must also try to contact the pupil's parents. The police should not interview anyone under the age of 17 without a parent, adult friend, or social worker being present.

Any pupil involved with unauthorised drugs at school runs the risk of being excluded. However, exclusion should not be automatic. The school should first look for other ways of dealing with the problem and exclusion should normally take place only after a thorough investigation – unless there is an immediate threat to the safety of the pupil concerned, or other pupils in school.

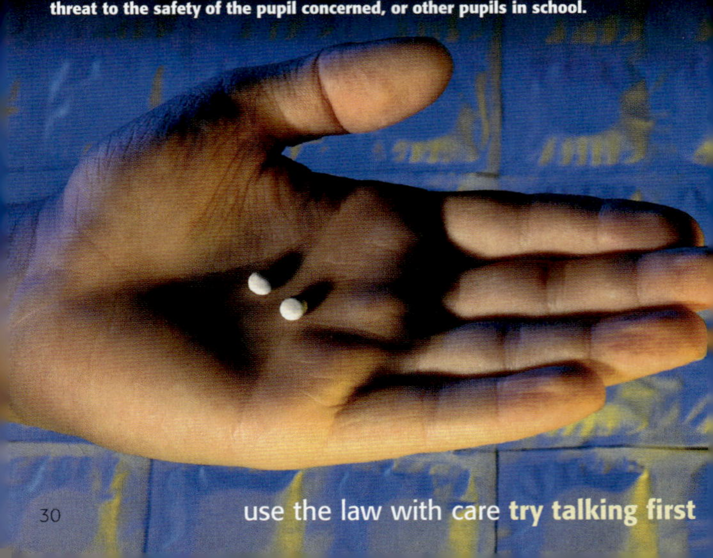

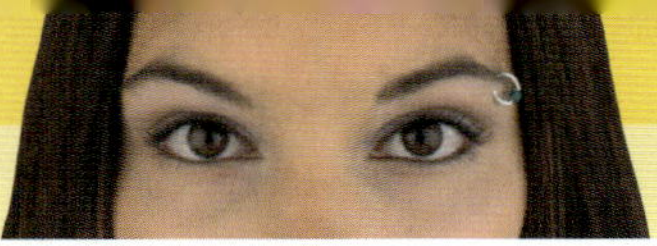

exclusion

A student who breaks an important school rule or commits a criminal offence in school may be excluded by the Head.

Fixed period or permanent?

A student may be excluded for a fixed period of time or permanently. Permanent exclusions are usually made only after a lot of disciplinary problems and when all other methods have been exhausted. They may also take place, however, if there is a serious breach of school rules – such as violent threats, assault, supplying an illegal drug or carrying an offensive weapon.

Students should not be excluded for one-off or minor incidents, like lateness, failing to do homework, or breaking rules on uniform or appearance – unless their behaviour is persistent and clearly in defiance of school rules.

A fixed period exclusion is for a set time and a Head may not exclude a student for more than 45 school days in a school year.

Procedure

Before a decision is taken to exclude a student, a thorough investigation of the circumstances surrounding the incident should take place – unless the Head feels that there is an immediate threat to the student or others in the school.

The student should be given the opportunity to give his or her version of the events, and their parents should be told of the exclusion without delay. They should receive a letter from the Head explaining the reasons for the exclusion, how long it will last, and how to appeal against it.

Powers and responsibilities

Under the *Education and Inspections Act 2006*, schools must set and mark work for a student from the sixth day of their exclusion. If a child is permanently excluded this becomes the responsibility of the local authority. When a student is excluded for a fixed period, the school has a duty to consider how the student should be reintegrated when their exclusion comes to an end, and how their problems might be addressed. In certain circumstances, this could mean applying to the court for a parenting order, which might require the student's mother or father to attend parenting classes or take other measures to improve their child's behaviour.

During the first five days of a student's exclusion, parents are now required to keep their child away from public places during school hours. If they do not, they may receive a fine.

reports and records

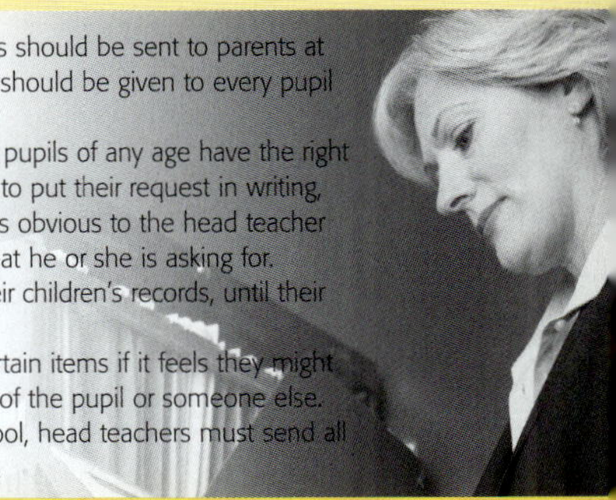

A written report on a student's progress should be sent to parents at least once a year and a leaver's report should be given to every pupil when they leave school.

Under the *Data Protection Act 1998*, pupils of any age have the right to see their school records. They need to put their request in writing, but this can be turned down only if it is obvious to the head teacher that the pupil does not understand what he or she is asking for.

Parents also have the right to see their children's records, until their child reaches 18.

However the school can withhold certain items if it feels they might damage the mental or physical health of the pupil or someone else.

When a pupil transfers to a new school, head teachers must send all educational records to the new school.

examinations

If a pupil is refused permission to sit a public exam, e.g. GCSE or A level, his or her parents may appeal to the school governors against this decision. A pupil, who has been entered for an exam, but fails to sit it without good reason, can be asked to pay the entry fee.

If a candidate does not do as well as expected in an exam, the school can ask for their paper to be checked, to make sure that the marks have been correctly assessed. Schools can also ask for a re-mark if it's felt that a serious mistake has been made in marking the paper. If the school remains dissatisfied, they can lodge an appeal with the Examinations Appeal Board. It is possible that compensation may be awarded if an examining board makes a serious error and this causes the student loss (for example, through deferral of a university place).

There is very little that can be done for a candidate who does badly in an exam because of poor teaching or a failure by a teacher to follow the correct procedure – or even the right syllabus. The examining board give grades based on the candidate's actual performance. Action through the courts for compensation can be extremely costly with no guarantee of success.

bullying

Schools have a legal duty to make sure students are safe in school, including on their journey to and from school. All schools must have an anti-bullying policy and policies protecting students from racial or sexual discrimination, and must act immediately on any evidence of a pupil being bullied. If they do not, they may be sued for negligence.

Schools are entitled to exclude pupils permanently who are persistent bullies and in serious cases may inform the police.

Childline provides a 24-hour telephone helpline, with trained counsellors able to talk to children and young people about bullying, tel 0800 1111.

Safety

Teachers take on some of the responsibilities of parents whilst pupils are in their care (known in law as being *in loco parentis*). On a school journey, this can apply for 24 hours a day. The standard of supervision required depends on the nature of the activity and the age or capability of the pupils. Where the action of teachers is called into question, the test the courts apply is whether they acted towards the pupils as careful parents would towards their own children.

BRIEF CASE: Bullying

Ten pupils, who bullied younger children at a school in Doncaster, were found guilty of a total of 39 charges – including blackmail, robbery, and assault. The three most prominent members of the gang were sentenced to four, six and eight months in a young offender institution.

School and college

Education Maintenance Allowance (EMA)

EMAs are financial payments designed to encourage students to stay in education after 16, and to help with the costs of their travel, books and equipment. Payments of £10, £20 or £30 a week are available during term time, depending on total household income.

Applicants must be aged between 16 and 18 and enrolled on specific full-time courses, such as GCSEs, A or AS levels, and certain diplomas or basic skills courses.

Students who apply for an EMA are required to sign a contract agreeing to good attendance. The money is paid directly into the student's bank or building society account, and bonuses are available to students who meet their attendance and performance targets. An EMA is not taxable and does not affect other benefits, but may be withdrawn or have to be paid back if a student fails to meet the terms of their learning agreement.

Other financial help

Students studying in the sixth form or at FE college may also be entitled to help from Discretionary Support Funds. These are designed to help students facing financial hardship. Details are available from local authorities, schools or colleges.

Students in Wales may apply for an Assembly Learning Grant (ALG), available to students aged 19 and over, studying on a course of at least 27.5 hours leading to a nationally recognised qualification. Payments are available up to £1,500 for full-time students and £750 for part-time students, and again depend on household income.

Young parents who are under 20, in further education and caring for their children can get help of up to £160 per week (£175 in London) with childcare and travel costs under the Care to Learn scheme. See **contacts** for further details.

Higher Education

There are two main areas of expenditure for students – the cost of their tuition, and general living costs.

Tuition fees

Students who start their course in England in September 2009 will be required to pay tuition fees of up to £3,225 a year. Students who live and study at college or university in Wales are entitled to a non-means tested grant of up to £1,940 to cover their fees, which does not have to be repaid. Students from Wales who choose to study outside their own country are generally required to pay the fees of the country in which they are studying.

Living costs

These are likely to be in the region of £6-9,000 a year, depending on where you live, your accommodation arrangements and your general spending patterns.

Help from the government

The availability of financial help from the government depends on the course you are taking, where you live, and your individual circumstances.

Tuition fees

A government loan is available to cover the cost of tuition fees. It does not depend on your family or household income, and becomes repayable when you have finished university and are earning more than £15,000 a year.

Maintenance grant

Students in England and Wales, from poorer backgrounds, may be entitled to financial help from a maintenance grant, currently worth up to £2,835 per year.

Students whose family income is below £25,000 per year receive the full grant. Those whose family income is between £25,000 and £60,005 receive a partial grant; although at the higher level, it is very small.

The maintenance grant is paid in three termly instalments, and does not need to be repaid.

Special Support Grant A Special Support Grant is available for students who are eligible to receive Income Support and other means-tested benefits such as Housing Benefit. It covers additional course costs such as books, equipment, travel or childcare. The arrangements for assessing and paying the special support grant are the same as for the maintenance grant, above.

A bank overdraft

Most banks offer special accounts for students, often with incentives such as vouchers, discounts or a free railcard. They also offer an overdraft facility (see **money** page 63) allowing you to go overdrawn up to a certain amount (sometimes up to £2,000 at the end of your course).

The interest rates on student overdraft are normally very low, but may rise sharply when your course is over.

Bursaries and scholarships

Many universities offer bursaries, designed to reduce the overall cost of fees. These are often specifically available for students whose families are on a low income, but may also be available to students who have achieved high grades at A level. Information is available from individual university websites. A national bursary scheme operates for students in Wales.

STUDENT LOANS

How much can I borrow? This depends on your family's income, whether you are living at or away from home, and whether you are studying in or outside London.

Currently (2008-9), students living away from home and studying outside London can obtain a maximum loan of £4,625, or £6,475 if their university or college is in London. The maximum for students from Wales studying in London is £6,480.

Students from England can also apply for a tuition fee loan of up to £3,225 a year (2009), depending on how much they are charged by their university. This loan does not depend on the size of their household income.

How much will the loan cost?

Interest is charged on the loan from the date on which the first payment is made, and is linked to the rate of inflation. It is currently three per cent.

When do I pay it back? You don't have to start paying it back until your course has finished, and you have a job in which you earn a least £15,000 per year. Deductions will be made automatically by your employer, in the same way as tax and insurance.

A person earning £1,500 per month (£18,000 per year) would have £22.50 deducted each month. Payments would cease if their annual income fell below £15,000, and begin again when it returned to a figure above this level.

If you wish, you may pay off your loan more quickly with extra voluntary repayments.

Where can I get more information?

Information is available from your local authority and from a number of websites, see contacts for details.

young citizen's **passport**

work and training

INDIVIDUALS ENGAGING IN SOCIETY

Citizenship Foundation

part-time work

At what age?

Certain laws that control the work of young people below school leaving age vary from one town or county to another. *Under the Children and Young Persons Act 1933*, each local authority creates its own by-laws giving the terms and conditions for the employment of young people in that area.

These state the kind of work that a young person may or may not do and require employers to inform the council of all young people they employ. Although ignored in many areas, the rules also state that, generally speaking, anyone below school leaving age who has a part-time job must have a medical certificate of fitness for work and an employment card issued by the local council.

The only kinds of employment children under 14 can be given are occasional light farm work, supervised by a parent, or parts in plays or films etc., for which a special licence is required from the local authority.

Children aged 14 or over may be employed only in light work approved by their local authority.

No young person below school leaving age may be employed before 7am or after 7pm, for more than one hour before the start of school, for more than twelve hours a week during term time, or for more than two hours on a school day (or on a Sunday).

A local authority licence is needed for someone aged between 14 and 16 to be paid to take part in sport.

There are few restrictions on the employment of 16 or 17 year olds. However, people under 18 cannot normally work in a bar, unless they work in a restaurant where drinks are served with meals, or are being trained for the licensing trade under a Modern Apprenticeship scheme. Copies of the by-laws controlling the employment of young people in your area can be obtained from the local library, or the local council website.

BRIEF CASE

A boy of 14, working in a factory making beds, suffered severe injuries when his arm was trapped in an unguarded machine. A court fined his employer £1,000 for failing to fit a guard to the machine and £200 for employing a child. The employer also paid £438 towards the costs of the case.

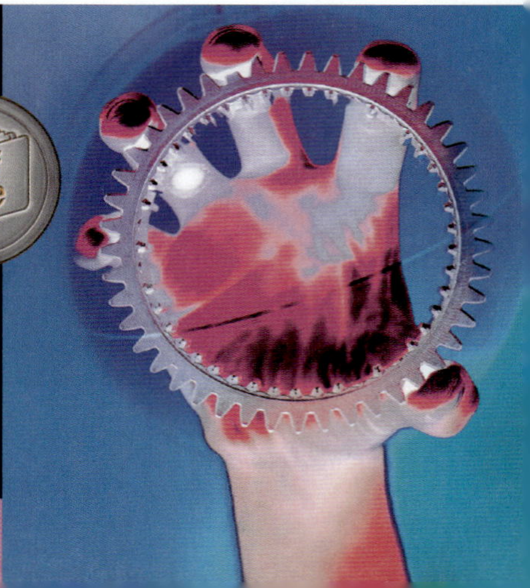

Employment rights

Today, many of the rights of those in part-time jobs (even if it's for only a couple of hours per week) are now the same as those of people in full-time employment.

If you are in part-time work you...

- **are protected by the anti-discrimination laws, regardless of how many hours you work or how long you have worked for your employer;**
- **have the right, if you have worked for your employer for one month, to be given notice if asked to leave and, after two months, to receive the terms and conditions of your job in writing;**
- **are entitled to redundancy pay if you are made redundant and have worked for your employer for at least two years;**
- **are entitled to claim for unfair dismissal if you have worked for your employer for at least a year, and feel you have been unfairly sacked.**

The *Part-time Workers (Prevention of Less Favourable Treatment) Regulations 2000* state that part-timers must receive the same treatment as full-time workers in relation to their hourly rates of pay, training, holiday, and maternity rights, etc.

training

Youth training

A training programme place is guaranteed to anyone aged 16 or 17 not in full-time education or work and can be offered to those in work. Places are also available to anyone aged between 18 and 24 who has not received training because of ill health, disability, language problems, pregnancy or through being in prison or in care. No one can remain on youth training after their 25th birthday. There is no residential requirement for youth training. A young homeless person is eligible for a training place in the same way as anyone else in their age group.

The pattern for youth training varies. It can be full or part-time and a mixture of on and off-the-job training.

If you decide to train in the workplace you will probably choose between a Foundation or an Advanced Modern Apprenticeship. In a Foundation Apprenticeship, you will work towards a National Vocational Qualification (NVQ) at level 2 (equivalent to one A level) focusing on a particular skill, e.g. information technology. You can go on to an Advanced Modern Apprenticeship and get an NVQ level 3 (equivalent to two A levels). Modern Apprenticeships are aimed at preparing for work at technician, craft or junior management level.

training

Pay

You may be taken on as an employee or a work-based trainee. As an employee, you will receive at least the minimum wage (see page 43). Apprentices do not qualify for the minimum wage until they are 19 or have completed a year of their apprenticeship, whichever comes later. If you are a trainee, you will receive a training allowance, which can be reduced for part-time work or unauthorised absences.

Terms and conditions

Whether you are an employee or a work-based trainee, you are entitled to receive written details of the terms and conditions of your training. If you are employed you are covered by all the other rights and benefits mentioned in this chapter.

You will also be given an individual training plan that will explain:

- **how your training will be organised;**
- **the dates when your programme begins and ends;**
- **your hours of work;**
- **details of the NVQ for which you are training.**

If you are not happy with your training, you may be able to transfer to a different programme with the same or a different trainer. If your trainer cannot finish your training, you should be given the opportunity to transfer to another trainer with a similar training programme.

If you are absent for more than the period specified in your terms and conditions, without permission from your trainer, your training programme will end.

Careers advisors, and your local Learning and Skills Council have details of apprenticeships in your area. Also see the Modern Apprenticeships website www.apprenticeships.org.uk

Equal opportunities

Trainees have the same protection as other workers against discrimination. Help is available at your careers office and the local Citizens Advice Bureau. For more information, see **equal rights**, page 46.

BRIEF CASE: Karen

Karen applied for an apprenticeship at a garage in Surrey. She was the best qualified applicant and had already worked in a garage as part of her work experience. At her interview she was asked whether she minded spending all day in a pair of dirty overalls, covered in oil and grease. Karen said she wasn't bothered, but didn't get the job. Karen believed she had been unfairly discriminated against on the grounds of her sex and took her case to an employment tribunal. The tribunal agreed and awarded just over £24,000 for loss of earnings and injury to her feelings.

Health & safety

Your trainer or employer must make sure that the place where you work is safe, and you have a legal responsibility to follow all safety procedures and use equipment in the way instructed.

If you have an accident, or are worried about safety, speak to your supervisor immediately. If you are injured or become ill while training, you should also contact your local Jobcentre Plus. You should continue to receive your training allowance for three weeks after an accident and then you will need to make a claim for Income Support.

Anyone injured on a government funded training scheme may be able to claim Disablement Benefit. Contact your local Jobcentre Plus for details.

Problems

When you start training you should be told what to do if you have any problems while on the programme. If you are unhappy with the training you can discuss it with your supervisor or see the careers officer, who may be able to help solve the problem or find you more suitable training.

Non-employed trainees are not entitled to any notice if they are dismissed, nor can they take their case to an employment tribunal if they feel they have been sacked unfairly. But if they are offered another job, they don't need to work out their notice before leaving. Employed trainees or apprentices receive the same legal protection as other employees and should give whatever period of notice is stated in their contract of employment.

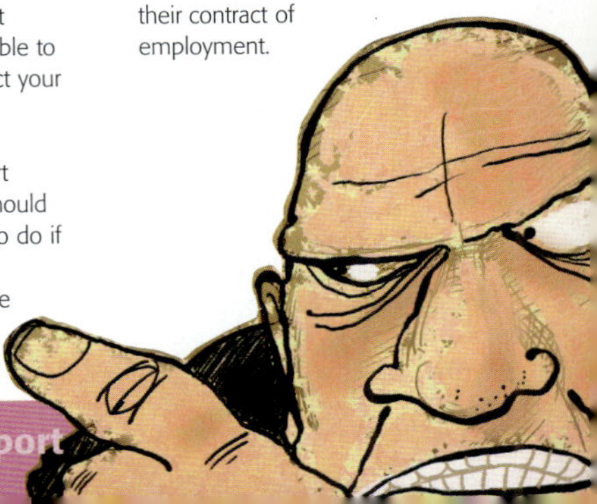

training

NEW DEAL

This programme is designed to help young people into work, with advice, support, training and work experience. It falls into two categories. The first is for people aged 18–24 who have been claiming Jobseeker's Allowance for six months or more. (Some people, such as lone parents, ex-offenders, those who have just left the armed services and those with a health condition or disability need not wait for the six month qualification period.) The second category is for long-term unemployed people, aged 25 and over.

New Deal for 18–24 year olds is compulsory in the sense that someone who doesn't take up the programme without good reason, stands to lose their right to benefits. If you are eligible, you will have an appointment with a personal adviser who will explain the programme, give you advice on finding work and monitor progress, based on an action plan that you will be required to draw up.

If, at the end of this initial period of up to four months, you are not yet in work, your personal adviser will arrange a package of help that might include training, work experience and help with applying for and obtaining work. During this time, you will receive a training allowance equivalent to your Jobseeker's Allowance plus a possible top-up payment of £15.38 per week. If you are on a training or work placement, you have the same legal rights as other employees – but no right to stay in the post after six months.

If you do not find work at the end of this period, you will continue to receive Jobseeker's Allowance and your personal adviser will carry on helping you to find a job.

Again, if you don't accept any of these alternatives or fail to turn up to interviews without giving a good reason, payment of your Jobseeker's Allowance is put at risk.

For more information about New Deal contact your local Job Centre Plus or see www.jobcentreplus.gov.uk.

applying for work

Applications

Read through the application form before starting to fill it in. Draft your longer answers in rough, until you are happy with what you have written.

All the information you give should be correct. An employer is entitled to dismiss someone who is deliberately misleading on their application form or at interview.

Your CV

Some adverts for jobs tell you to send for an application form, others will ask for a letter with your curriculum vitae, usually known as a CV. This is something that you write or type, giving personal details, qualifications, experience, and interests. Make several copies and don't forget to keep one for yourself.

Referees

You will need the names of two people who are prepared to act as your referees, to write a short report or reference about you for an employer. One referee is usually your last employer, or the head teacher or year tutor in your school. References must be factually accurate and should not create a misleading or unfair impression of the person concerned.

Interviews

If you've not been to the office or building before, leave yourself extra time to find it; or go round and find out where it is beforehand. If you can't make the appointment, phone or write to explain and ask for a more convenient time.

Have a few questions ready to ask – about what the course or job involves. If they offer you a place or job, before you accept try to think if there's anything else you need to know. If there is, ask.

Everyone at work has a contract – whether full or part-time, permanent or fixed term.

A contract is another word for the agreement between you and your employer, spelling out the arrangements that will affect your work – such as pay, hours, the sort of job you will do, holidays and the notice you have to give, or you can expect to receive, when your employment comes to an end.

Terms and conditions in writing

If you are to be employed for more than one month, your employer must give you a written statement within two months of starting work, setting out the terms and conditions of your job.

This statement should give...

- **your job title and place of work;**
- **your starting date;**
- **your rate of pay, and details of how and when you will be paid;**
- **your hours of work;**
- **your holidays and holiday pay;**
- **arrangements for sick pay and pension;**
- **details of the firm's disciplinary procedures and how complaints at work are dealt with;**
- **the amount of notice that you or your employer must give if your contract is to be ended.**

Apart from your written statement, the terms of your employment do not have to be in writing. They can be agreed verbally – but it's a good idea to have things in writing, in case there's disagreement about what you're expected to do.

Check your contract carefully. Make sure you agree with what it says and that it covers everything you are being asked to do. If it is different from the agreement made at your interview, point this out. Keep safe all pay slips, letters and papers you are given by your employer.

Take care

If you agree to do something on a regular basis that is not written into your contract – like working on a Saturday – you may be, in law, agreeing to a new term or condition of work. If you decide later that working every Saturday is not a good idea, your boss may be entitled to insist that you continue. By turning up for work six days a week, you may have actually changed your contract by your conduct.

Pay

Your wages will either be agreed between you and your boss or else based on rates agreed between employers and trade unions. Either way, your employer must give you a detailed written pay statement showing exactly what you are earning and how much is being taken off in tax, national insurance, etc. It is up to your employer to choose how you are paid. This can be by cash, cheque, or straight into your bank account.

Your rate of sick pay must be explained in your contract. It may say that you will be paid at your standard rate for a certain length of time, or that you will be given statutory sick pay. This is set each year by the Department for Work and Pensions and is usually lower than your normal pay. If you are off sick for four or more days in a row (including Sundays and bank holidays) you will receive statutory sick pay from your employer for up to 28 weeks. You don't have to claim statutory sick pay, just follow your employer's rules for notifying sickness.

You can check what you should receive in leaflets available from Social Security offices and libraries.

Hours

Your hours of work will normally be agreed between you and your employer, although there are some jobs where these are limited by law for reasons of health and safety.

The *Working Time Regulations* set a maximum working week of 48 hours, including overtime, calculated over 17 weeks for workers aged 18 and over. You can agree to do more than this, but your employer cannot pressurise you to do so. You are also entitled to:

- **a rest break of 20 minutes when you work for more than 6 hours at a time (or 30 minutes when you work for more than 4½ hours if you are under 18);**
- **at least 11 consecutive hours off in any 24 hour period (12 hours off, if you are under 18).**

Workers who are over school leaving age but under 18 may not work more than 8 hours a day or 40 hours a week. Nor may they ordinarily work between 10pm and 6am. Some night work is allowed in certain jobs, such as the armed forces, farm work, catering, work in a pub, restaurant or hotel, work in a bakery, newspaper delivery and retail trading. However, an adult must supervise the work and rest periods must be given. If you believe that the hours you are expected to work do not follow the regulations, raise the issue with your employer. If this fails, you can then take your case to an employment tribunal.

THE MINIMUM WAGE

Under the *National Minimum Wage Act 1998*, all employees must be paid a minimum wage, which varies according to their age. From October 2008, the minimum rate payable to 16 and 17-year-olds, who are above compulsory school age, is £3.53 per hour. For people aged 18–21, it is £4.77 an hour, and £5.73 for 22-year-olds and above, unless they are in the first six months of a new job or on an accredited training course. If you are being paid less than the national minimum wage, you have a legal right to raise the matter with your manager and get in touch with your trade union, if you are a member.

An employer can be fined for paying below the minimum wage and must not treat an employee unfairly for raising the subject.

If your employer fails to grant your legal rights, you may take your case to an employment tribunal. Further help is available from the National Minimum Wage Helpline and the Inland Revenue, see contacts for details.

Rules and regulations

Internet and e-mail

Under the *Human Rights Act 1998* and the *Regulation of Investigatory Powers Act 2000*, employers are entitled to set reasonable rules for their workers who use e-mail and the internet at work.

They can forbid employees from writing or reading personal e-mails or browsing websites for personal interest during work time, and can monitor what they do. However, employees should be informed that checks of this kind might be made. An employer who opens an employee's e-mails without a good business reason could well be infringing that person's right to privacy and respect for family life (see **human rights**, page 132).

E-mail files may however be opened without an employee's consent in extreme circumstances, to check, for example, whether the law has been broken.

HOLIDAYS

Since April 2009, the *Working Time Regulations* give most people over 16, who are in full-time work, the right to a minimum of 28 days' paid holiday a year (including eight bank holidays). If you work on a part-time basis, your holiday entitlement will be reduced proportionately. During the first year of employment, you have the right to take one twelfth of your annual holiday entitlement for each month worked. Some jobs are not covered by the Regulations, for example those in the transport and fishing industries, the police, and armed forces.

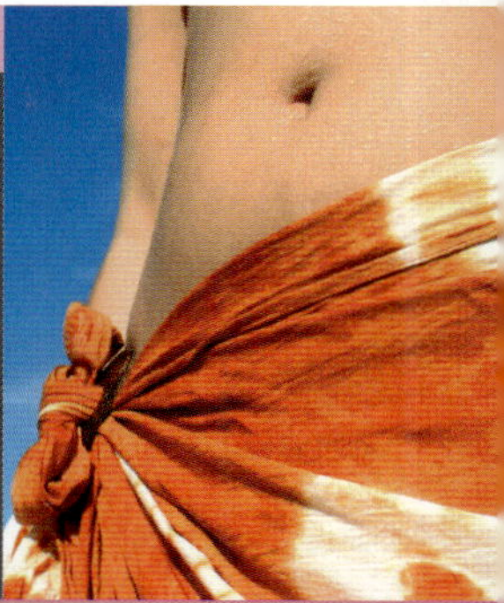

health and safety

Safety

Employers have a legal duty to take care of the safety of their staff. If they don't, they are breaking the *Health and Safety at Work Act 1974*.

This means that the equipment that you use must not be dangerous or defective, and that the people you work with must work safely and responsibly.

Your duty is to follow safety regulations and instructions and to take care of your own and other people's safety.

If you work for a firm where there are five or more employees, your boss must give you details of the health and safety arrangements in writing.

If you are worried about health and safety, raise the matter with your supervisor. Your employer may not dismiss you or treat you unfairly for raising genuine concerns, as long as you follow the right procedures. If you remain concerned, contact the local offices of the Health and Safety Executive. Your local Citizens Advice Bureau will be able to tell you how to do this.

BRIEF CASE: Maria

Maria worked as a waitress in a holiday centre in North Wales. Her staff chalet was in poor condition, with mould growing on the walls, no heating, and a very dirty mattress.

One morning Maria felt unwell, and noticed a rash on her right arm. She went to the doctor who said that the rash had been caused by insect bites, possibly flees.

Maria complained to her boss who arranged for her accommodation to be decontaminated. When Maria moved back a few days later she was again bitten and once more complained.

Shortly afterwards, Maria was dismissed, being told that the centre was over-staffed. Maria thought this was unfair; believing that the real reason she had lost her job was her complaint about health and safety. An employment tribunal agreed, saying that her dismissal had almost certainly been triggered by the health concerns she had raised. Maria was awarded compensation for unfair dismissal.

BRIEF CASE: Gary

Gary, 18, worked in a butcher's and was cutting meat when his hand slipped and he cut off the top of two fingers. His boss had often told him to use a special guard – but most people at work ignored this, so Gary didn't bother either. Gary was awarded damages in court because his employer did not make sure that he was working in the right way, but they were reduced by a third because he hadn't followed the safety instructions.

Accidents

If you are injured at work, report the matter to your supervisor straightaway and, unless the injury is very small, see a doctor. Make a note of what happened, check to see whether you are entitled to any welfare benefits and get legal advice from either your trade union, your local Citizens Advice Bureau, Law Centre or a solicitor. You may be entitled to compensation for your injuries.

Using a computer screen

If you have a problem with your eyes that you think might be due to using display screen equipment at work, your employer has a duty to arrange for you to have an eyesight test if you ask for one, and to do whatever they reasonably can at work to reduce further problems. This is all part of a general requirement for employers to check on the health and safety risks to people using computer screens at work, contained in the *Health and Safety (Display Screen Equipment) Regulations 1992*.

Discrimination Over the last 40 years, the law has gradually provided more and more protection against discrimination at work. Discrimination law applies to all aspects of work including applications, terms and conditions of work, conduct in the workplace and references that might be given when you have left.

Sex Under the *Sex Discrimination Act 1975*, it is against the law to treat a person less favourably because of their sex. In addition, the *Equal Pay Act 1970* gives women and men rights to equal pay for the same or similar work. A few jobs are excluded. These include acting, modelling, and those that may involve physical or close contact with the opposite sex.

Race It is against the law to discriminate against someone because of their colour, race, nationality, or ethnic origin. This is covered by the *Race Relations Act 1976*, and applies equally to all racial groups.

There are certain circumstances when race discrimination is not against the law. The law does not cover employment in private households or when a person's race or ethnic group is seen as a 'genuine occupational qualification', such as in a restaurant serving food from a particular country or region.

Disability It is against the law, under the *Disability Discrimination Act 1995*, for any employer to treat a person less favourably on grounds of their disability, or for a reason related to their disability, unless the treatment can be justified. Employers are also required to make reasonable adjustments to the working environment in order to enable a person with disabilities to be employed.

BRIEF CASE: Overlooked

Three Asian men, who worked at a paper mill in Burnley, were continually passed over for promotion in favour of white colleagues. When the men asked why, they were told they would not be effective in more senior positions. They took their case to an employment tribunal, which heard that the men frequently faced racist insults and banter, which supervisors did nothing to stop.

The tribunal agreed that the three workers had suffered race discrimination, and awarded them a total of £47,000 in compensation for loss of earnings and damage to their feelings. The company was also required to change its working practices so that no further discrimination took place.

BRIEF CASE: Eugene

Eugene suffered constant racist taunts from other workers on the building site where he worked, and the management did little to stop it. They said that 'black bastard' and 'nigger' were words often used on sites. The tribunal decided that Eugene had suffered unlawful discrimination. He was awarded £2,000 damages.

Religion Under the *Employment Equality (Religion or Belief) Regulations 2003*, employers must not treat an employee less favourably than others because of their religion or belief. Nor should employers have rules and practices that put someone at a disadvantage because of their religion or belief. For example, employers generally do not have the right to compel a person to dress in a particular way that is against their religion or system of belief, unless there is a justifiable reason to do so (for example, health and safety).

Sexuality Since 2003, it has been against the law to discriminate against someone at work because of their sexuality or perceived sexuality. Under the *Employment Equality (Sexual Orientation) Regulations 2003*, employers may not treat gay, lesbian, heterosexual or bisexual employees less favourably than others of a different sexuality.

Age It is now against the law to discriminate against someone at work because of their age. Generally speaking, a person should not be turned down for a job because they are too old or too young, and employers should not advertise jobs for particular age groups or in a way that discourages candidates in particular age groups from applying.

Help and advice If you feel you have been a victim of discrimination at work, you can get help from your local Citizens Advice Bureau, Law Centre, trade union or from a solicitor. Advice and information on most matters of discrimination on the grounds of race, sex, disability, religion, age or sexual orientation is available from the Equality and Human Rights Commission, see **contacts**.

If you can't sort things out directly with your employer, you may be advised to take your complaint to an employment tribunal. This must normally be done within three months (or six months, if it is a claim under the *Equal Pay Act*). If you win, the tribunal can award damages to compensate you for any financial losses you have suffered and any injury to feelings. You may be able to settle your case without the need to go to an employment tribunal but, if not, be prepared for a long and difficult battle, and remember to take legal advice.

BRIEF CASE: Susan

Susan, a train driver on the London Underground, was forced to hand in her notice when new shift rosters meant that it was impossible for her to work and look after her three-year-old child. She took her case to an employment tribunal, complaining of sex discrimination. The tribunal decided that the new working arrangements indirectly discriminated against women because more women were single parents.

Harassment at work

The law also allows employees to make a claim against their employer if they face harassment at work. Like discrimination, this can be because of their sex, race, disability, religion or belief, sexual orientation or age.

Harassment refers to unwanted behaviour towards someone that they find intimidating, offensive or demeaning. Examples might include:

- **unwanted advances or physical contact;**
- **insulting remarks;**
- **comments on a person's looks.**

It is an employer's duty to take steps to prevent these kinds of things from happening. If you face difficulties of this kind it's usually better, if you can, to try to sort things out informally. But if the harassment continues, don't be afraid to complain using your employer's grievance procedure. It's not always easy to prove in court, but judges are prepared to award damages when the victim can show that they have suffered some financial disadvantage and/or injury to their feelings from the harassment.

BRIEF CASE

An employment tribunal decided that a secretary, who was sacked when she complained about being groped by a senior member of staff at a Christmas party, was unfairly dismissed. She was awarded £4,700 in damages.

BRIEF CASE: Offensive and degrading

Janine worked with a group of men who regularly looked at pornographic sites on their computers at work. Their boss knew this was going on, but did nothing to stop it – even though Janine had told him that it made her feel very uncomfortable. Eventually Janine made a complaint of sexual harassment to an employment tribunal. The tribunal decided that the men's behaviour was degrading and offensive to women and that the employer should have taken steps to stop it, and ordered the company to pay Janine compensation for the damage she had suffered.

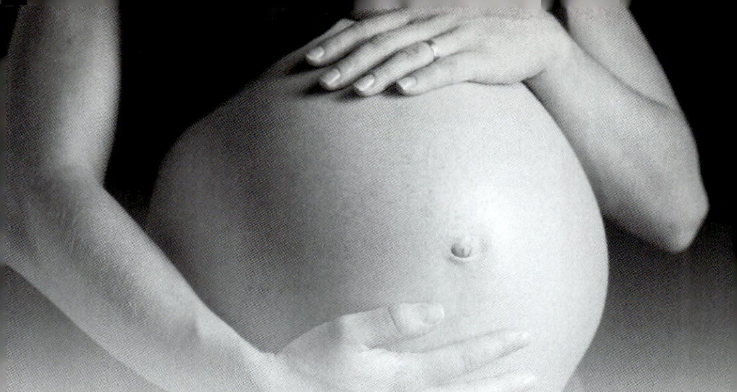

maternity and family rights

Maternity rights

Female employees who are expecting a baby or adopting a child have certain minimum legal rights (although some employers provide more than these). Your contract or staff handbook should give you details. Employees in this situation should not be treated less favourably at work for any reason connected with their pregnancy or decision to adopt.

Time off with pay for antenatal care

This applies to full and part-time employees, and it makes no difference how long you have worked for your employer. Your employer cannot insist that you make up the time, or that you take the appointment in your free time.

Maternity leave

Pregnant women are entitled to 52 weeks of maternity leave; no matter how long they have worked for their employer, and whether they are full or part-time. They also have the right to return to the same, or similar, job after their maternity leave is over.

All benefits listed in your contract, except pay, continue during your maternity leave – including, for example, medical insurance and a company car, if you have one. You can agree to work for up to ten days during your maternity leave to keep in touch with your workplace.

Correct procedures

If you don't follow the correct procedures in applying for maternity leave, you risk losing the right to return to your job after your baby is born or your right to maternity pay. For example, you must give notice to your employer by the end of the 15th week before the baby is due. The personnel department at work, your trade union, local Citizens Advice Bureau, or Law Centre can explain what you need to do.

Maternity pay

You are entitled to maternity pay for the first 39 weeks of your maternity leave including the time you take off before your baby is born, provided you have worked for your employer for a sufficient length of time. Your maternity pay will probably be lower than your usual rate, unless it says otherwise in your contract. If you are on a low income, or have not worked for long enough to qualify for maternity pay, you may still be entitled to a maternity allowance from the Benefits Agency.

The standard rate of maternity pay and the maternity allowance is £117.18 per week (2008/9), or 90 per cent of your average weekly earnings, if less.

maternity and family rights

Paternity leave

A father has a right to take up to two weeks' paid paternity leave. This must be taken in one block and is only available to employees who have worked for 26 continuous weeks for their employer. Statutory paternity pay is paid at the same rate as standard statutory maternity pay.

Parental leave

Both parents can each take up to 13 weeks' unpaid parental leave over the first five years of their child's life and in blocks of up to four weeks a year, provided they have worked for their employer for at least a year. Parents of disabled children are entitled to 18 weeks' unpaid leave over the first 18 years of the child's life.

Time off

Regardless of how long you have worked for your employer, you have the right to take unpaid time off for urgent family problems, such as an accident or the sudden illness of someone who depends on you for their care, but you must give your employer the reasons for your absence as soon as possible. You may only take a reasonable amount of time. If your employer refuses, you can complain to an employment tribunal.

Right to request flexible working

If you have 26 weeks' continuous service and are a parent, step-parent, adoptive parent, foster carer or guardian of a child who is under six years old or a disabled child who is under 18 years old, you have the right to request flexible working hours for the purpose of looking after your child. Adults caring for their spouses, parents or, partners can also request flexible working hours.

trade unions

Membership

It is up to you whether you join a trade union. Trade unions don't only negotiate wages for their members. They also give advice, inform members of their rights and act on their behalf over difficulties with their employer. An employer must not sack someone for either belonging or not belonging to a trade union.

Not all employers want to work with unions. But, if there are more than 20 people working for an employer, a trade union may be able to force the employer to recognise the union and to negotiate with them.

Industrial action

If you take industrial action – for example, by stopping work – you may be breaking your contract. However, if the strike has been lawfully organised and correctly balloted, your employer is not entitled to dismiss you for taking part. If it does so, this is automatically unfair and you may have a case for compensation. But you cannot claim unfair dismissal if you are sacked for taking part in an unofficial strike.

losing your job

If you're sacked or made redundant, your legal rights mainly depend on how long you have been working for your employer.

Notice Unless you have done something very serious and committed what's known in law as gross misconduct – such as theft or fighting – your boss should not sack you on the spot. Your contract should state the notice to which you are entitled, and this usually depends on how long you have been working for your employer.

After one month's employment, either side should give one week's notice. After two years' employment, your employer should give you two weeks' notice, three weeks' after three years, and so on, up to a maximum of 12 weeks' notice for employment which has lasted 12 years or more.

However, your notice period might be longer if this is stated in your contract, and your employer may decide to pay you instead of letting you work out your notice. Before dismissing you, your employer must follow certain procedures, designed to promote discussion about your position.

Reasons in writing If you are fired by your employer, for whom you have worked for more than one year, you can ask for a written statement of the reasons for your dismissal, which must be provided within 14 days.

Redundancy This happens when an employer no longer needs the job done for which you were employed. Your rights mainly depend on your age and how long you have worked for the firm.

If you are made redundant, you have a right to redundancy pay, if you…

- **have worked for your employer for a continuous period of at least two years; and**
- **have not unreasonably turned down an offer of another job from your employer.**

If your employer has gone bust, you may be able to get a redundancy payment from the Redundancy Payments Service.

If you are made redundant, get advice from your trade union, Citizens Advice Bureau, Law Centre or a solicitor as soon as possible. If you feel that the way you were chosen for redundancy was unfair or unreasonable, or that your employer has failed to consult adequately with you, you may also be able to claim unfair dismissal.

UNFAIR DISMISSAL

If you have been dismissed, and feel that your employer has acted unfairly or failed to follow a set procedure, you can make a complaint to an employment tribunal. You normally need one year's service to bring a claim.

You may also have a claim for unfair dismissal if you leave your job because of your employer's behaviour. This is known in law as constructive dismissal, but will only be successful if you can show that your employer has broken your employment contract. If you are thinking of resigning because of this, keep a record of what is happening and, before you hand in your notice, write to your employer explaining your reasons for leaving.

Take legal advice before you make a claim for unfair dismissal. Your trade union, local Citizens Advice Bureau, Law Centre or a solicitor can help. If you are unhappy about your dismissal, don't delay in seeking assistance. **You normally only have three months in which to make a complaint.**

If the tribunal agrees that your dismissal was unfair, your employer will probably be ordered to pay you a sum in compensation. This is a basic award, which is calculated on the basis of your age, weekly pay and length of service, plus a figure for compensation. The maximum unfair dismissal basic award is £10,500 and the maximum figure for compensation is £66,200 (2009).

There are no limits to the damages you can receive if you lose your job as a result of discrimination or, for example for reasons such as health and safety.

BRIEF CASE: Sacked!

Jeannette's son was ill in the night and Jeannette overslept the next morning. When she arrived late at the video rental company where she worked, she was sacked. She explained what had happened, but her boss took no notice. Jeannette took her case to an employment tribunal, who decided that she had been unfairly dismissed, as she had not been given a warning or a second chance.

BRIEF CASE: Redundant!

Business was bad and Dean was made redundant from his job at a petrol station. He was given £520 redundancy pay, but soon realised that his job was now being done by the boss's son. Dean's job hadn't been redundant at all. He won his claim for unfair dismissal.

young citizen's passport

money

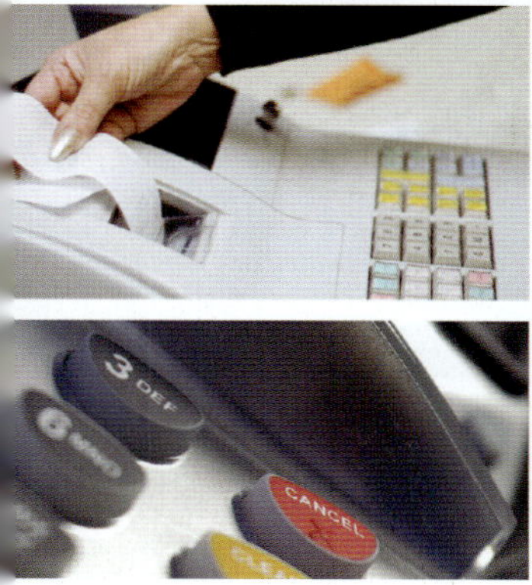

INDIVIDUALS ENGAGING IN SOCIETY

Citizenship Foundation

It's a contract

When you buy something from a shop or pay for a service (like a train fare or haircut) you are making an agreement, known in law as a *contract*.

The contract means that, in return for the money that you pay, the goods you buy should do everything you can reasonably expect and, in particular, all that the seller and manufacturer claim.

Once a contract has been agreed, neither side can change it on their own. Some shops allow customers to opt out of their contract by agreeing to exchange unwanted items or by providing a refund, as long as goods are returned in mint condition with the receipt. Shops don't have to do this by law, unless it was promised as part of the contract.

But what about your rights if the goods you have bought are faulty?

The Sale of Goods Act

The law applying to most everyday purchases is the *Sale of Goods Act 1979* – an important act that has been extended over the last 30 years. It says that when you buy goods from a shop or trader, they must…

…be of satisfactory quality

This means that they must be free from faults and not scratched or damaged, and equally applies to goods bought in a sale. However, this rule does not apply if the fault was pointed out by the sales assistant or if you inspected the item and had a good opportunity to discover the fault.

Second-hand goods bought from a shop or trader must also be of satisfactory quality.

…be fit for all their intended purposes

This means that they must do what the seller, packaging or advertisements claim. A watch sold as waterproof should not stop if you forget to take it off in the shower.

These protections do not apply if you bought the goods privately (e.g. through a 'small ad') – when the buyer is responsible for deciding the quality of what she or he wants to buy.

…match the description

The goods must be the same as the description on the packaging, or advertisement or given by the assistant at the time of sale. A bracelet marked solid silver, must be just that.

This rule also applies to second-hand goods, and goods sold privately.

GETTING IT RIGHT

If you're buying something expensive, it is wise to do some research beforehand. There are various consumer magazines and websites which review/rate different products. You can also go to a shop and ask just to see an item, without buying it. If you decide to make a purchase, keep the receipt in case you have a complaint.

Services too

Dry cleaners, shoe repairers, hairdressers, travel agents and many others provide a service – and you are protected by law if that service is inadequate.

Under the *Supply of Goods and Services Act 1982*, a service must be provided...

- **with reasonable care and skill;**
- **within a reasonable time; and**
- **for a reasonable charge, where it is not agreed beforehand.**

Problems?

Problems are less likely to occur if certain things are agreed before the work is started. How much will it cost? How long will it take? What happens if the work can't be finished? Try to sort these out first.

Handle your complaint just as you would were it for faulty goods. Don't be afraid to seek advice. Help is available from your local Citizens Advice Bureau, trading standards or consumer advice centre.

Some trades, such as travel agents, garages, dry cleaners, shoe sellers etc., have their own associations laying down a code of practice or standards. These have no legal standing, but the associations can help you resolve your complaint against a trader. Contact addresses are available from your local library or the internet.

Junk mail and phone calls

Junk mail

If you want to cut down on the junk mail you receive you can register with the *Mailing Preference Service* **www.mpsonline.org.uk**. It's quite a simple process, but takes about four months to take full effect.

Telesales

If you are worried, angered or inconvenienced by telesales calls, you can sign up to the *Telephone Preference Service,* **www.tpsonline.org.uk**, which screens and reduces the number of calls you will receive.

Spam

Most spam offers are a scam. If the message looks doubtful, delete it and don't click on the adverts. Under the *Privacy and Electronic Communications Regulations 2003*, UK businesses can send direct marketing messages by e-mail only to existing customers or to those people who have agreed to let them do so.

However, a great deal of bulk spam is sent from outside the UK, and there is little that UK law can do to deal with this. For further information, see **contacts**.

Rogue-dialling scams

Rogue dialling scams use a computer programme to trick victims' computers into dialling premium rate numbers, often costing as much as £1.50 per minute. Internet users can find that their telephone bill has increased by several hundred pounds after unknowingly downloading a rogue dial-up programme. Unfortunately, they have little choice but to pay up. Contacting your telephone provider and PhonepayPlus (see **contacts**) may stop the problem from happening again.

PUT DOWNS

Some businesses will do as much as they can to help you with a problem over something you have bought; others may claim that there is nothing they can do. Don't give up if the shop tries to get out of its legal obligations...

...we'll send it back to the workshop

Only if you want to. If you act reasonably quickly, you can choose whether to ask for a full or partial refund, compensation or to have the goods repaired or replaced (if that is a practical option). If the goods have developed a fault in the first six months it is assumed they were faulty when you bought them, unless the shop can prove otherwise.

... you'll have to take it up with the manufacturer

Wrong. You bought the goods from the shop and your contract was with them, not with a manufacturer on the other side of the world. If the goods genuinely don't work, the shop has not kept its side of the contract and you have a right to your money back. Shops normally have to accept responsibility to you for the manufacturer's claims. If the shop refuses to help, you can also use the guarantee to bring a claim against the manufacturer of the product.

...we'll give you a credit note

No. If the goods are faulty, you're entitled to your money back, providing you act quickly. You don't have to accept a credit note if you don't want to. If you do accept a credit note, check where and when you can use it – some credit notes must be used within a fixed time and only in exchange for certain goods or services.

...sorry, it's out of guarantee

This can be tricky. A major problem with an expensive computer three months after the guarantee has run out means a large repair bill. Raise it with the dealer and ask to talk to the manager. Produce the documentation and use the manufacturer's literature (which probably stresses reliability and quality) to point out that it is not reasonable to expect a failure after such a short period. There's no hard and fast law about what is reasonable in terms of a product failure. It depends on the circumstances.

...we don't give refunds on sale goods

Wrong. Unless the fault was pointed out to you or was something you should have seen when you bought them, goods bought in sales carry all the legal protection described above.

...we'll give you a replacement

Only if that's what you want. However, if by now the fault has led you to decide that you don't really want the product after all, you are entitled to your money back – not a replacement. It's up to you to choose what to do.

The small claims court

If you cannot get any satisfaction over a problem with faulty goods or poor service, you can write to the person concerned warning them that you will try to recover the money they owe you by taking your case to the small claims court (strictly known as the small claims track). This is a simplified way of settling disputes, in which a judge hears your case without you having to be represented by lawyers. Cases involve claims of less than £5,000 and can be brought only by someone of 18 or over. You can get more details from your local county court (under Courts in the phone book), the Citizens Advice Bureau or a consumer advice centre, see **contacts**.

Finding it's wrong

If you are not satisfied with something that you have bought…

- **Stop using it straightaway and take it back, with the receipt and guarantee (if you have one), to the shop where you bought it. It strengthens your case if you can do this as soon as possible. Your contract was with the shop, not the manufacturer, so it is the shop's responsibility to deal with your complaint. Even if you have lost the receipt, the contract still exists.**
- **Before you take the goods back, decide what you are going to say and what you would like the shop to do. Do you want your money back, or will you accept a repair or replacement item?**
- **Think about your legal position. A faulty earphone connection on an MP3 player means that it is not of satisfactory quality. Don't be afraid to use the law when making your case.**
- **If the shop assistant doesn't help, ask for someone more senior.**
- **If you bought the goods by mail order or from a shop some distance away, it's easier to telephone or write. Keep a copy of all letters, send a photocopy of your receipt (keep the original), and if you talk on the phone get the name of the person you spoke to. Make a brief note of the conversation.**

use the law with care **try talking first**

Buying over the phone or on the internet

If you buy goods online or over the phone, your basic legal rights are the same as buying something in a shop. However you also have a number of additional rights. These include the right to:

- **be given clear information about the nature of the product, what it will cost you (including taxes and delivery), and the name and address of the seller;**
- **cancel your order up to seven days after you have received the goods (see below);**
- **have the goods delivered within 30 days of your order, unless you agreed with the seller that it would take longer. If the goods do not arrive within this time, you are entitled to a full refund.**

Cancellation

The above rights to cancel do not apply to certain goods and services, including food and other perishable items, unsealed computer software, CDs and DVDs etc, magazines, newspapers and tickets for travel, accommodation or events. For further details contact your local Citizens Advice Bureau or the OFT website, see **contacts**.

Buying goods from outside the UK

If you are buying goods from a country within the EU (see the **European Union**, page 142) your basic legal rights may be different from those in the England and Wales. Your additional rights should be the same as they are in the UK. However, not all countries may yet have put them into practice and chasing up a supplier in another country may not be straightforward.

If you are buying from outside the EU, check the small print and be aware that the law may be different from the UK, which is likely to make it more difficult to pursue a complaint.

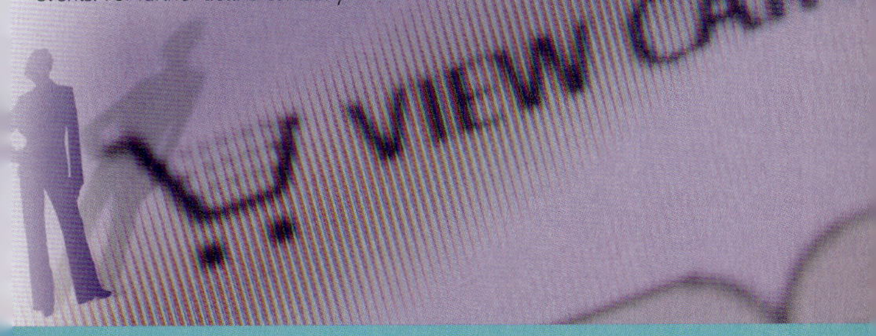

banks and building societies

Although there is no minimum legal age for someone to have a bank account, most banks offer basic accounts to young people aged eleven and over. These provide a cash card, which you can use at a bank machine to withdraw cash, and possibly a debit card that will only work if there's enough money in your account. A regular current account is normally available only if you are 18 or over (or 16 or 17 with a steady income or an adult who will act as guarantor).

WHY HAVE AN ACCOUNT?

- **many employers will only pay wages into an account;**
- **an account is needed for a student loan;**
- **the money can earn interest;**
- **regular accounts come with a cheque book and card to pay for things;**
- **you can pay cheques other people give you into an account.**

CHOOSING A BANK OR BUILDING SOCIETY

You will probably want to know:

- **whether it has a branch near you and offers on-line banking;**
- **whether there are convenient cash points;**
- **about services offered and charges;**
- **what interest is paid on the money in your account. There will be leaflets on this, or you can ask a member of staff;**
- **about special offers for young people.**

Don't be persuaded by offers or gifts if the services and charges are not as good as other banks or building societies.

There are two main types of accounts – current accounts and savings accounts.

Current accounts

A current account is for day-to-day transactions. You pay in money, such as your wages or student loan, which you can draw out as you please. If you are 18 or over, you usually get a chequebook and a cheque guarantee card, which allows you to pay for and take away things, with a signed cheque.

You'll receive a regular bank statement – usually every month – showing the amounts that have been paid in and withdrawn from your account and your overall balance.

Cheque books and guarantee cards

A cheque book contains a number of cheques with your name on. The person you give a cheque to pays it into their bank account, and after a few days the money is taken (debited) from your account and added (or credited) to their's.

If you haven't got enough money in your current account to cover the value of the cheque you have written, the bank may refuse to honour your cheque and it will bounce.

You may also be given a cheque guarantee card. This guarantees that the bank will pay your cheque up to the amount stated on the card – usually £50 or £100. If there isn't enough money in your account to

cover the value of the cheques you have written with your cheque guarantee card, you'll go overdrawn and may have to pay bank charges and interest. Strictly speaking, it is an offence to write a cheque when you know there is not enough money in your account to cover it, unless you have the permission of your bank to do so. Don't keep your cheque book and guarantee card together – if they are stolen this makes it easier to defraud you.

Cash cards These allow you to take money out of your current account from a cash machine, using a confidential personal identification number (PIN). Never keep a record of this number with your card. If your PIN number or card is stolen, contact your bank immediately.

Debit cards Your debit card allows you to buy things without writing a cheque or using cash. There is no legal age limit for obtaining a debit card, but as a rule banks tend to wait until their customers are 16 years old. You can also use it to pay for goods over the telephone or online. Your account is automatically debited with the amount you have spent. However, it can take a while (sometimes a few days) for payments to show on your balance. You can only go overdrawn with a debit card if you have the bank's agreement, otherwise you will be charged a fee. Many debit cards double as a cheque guarantee and cash card.

Pre-paid cards Users load the pre-paid card with money, and can only spend what they have on the card – this makes it impossible to go overdrawn. A fee is charged on most cards.

What do I do if someone gives me a cheque? Look to see that it is correctly written – that it is for the right amount, that it has been signed, and is not 'post-dated' (has a future date on).

Pay the cheque into your account as soon as possible, using a paying-in slip. Banks do not usually accept cheques more than six months old.

banks and building societies

Savings accounts

A savings account normally provides a higher rate of interest. Most do not come with a cheque book or plastic card, and some have restrictions on when you can withdraw your money. You will still be able to take out your money if your really have to, but will probably lose some of the extra interest.

If you keep money in your savings account while you are overdrawn on your current account or have a loan, you may find the interest you are paying is higher than the interest that you earn on your savings account.

What about tax on the interest I earn?

Interest earned on bank and building society accounts is usually paid after tax has been deducted from it. Unless you have a high income, that is normally the end of the matter, and there is no more tax to pay; see **tax** page 68. If you are not a taxpayer (because your earnings are not high enough), you can either get the tax back by contacting a tax office or you can choose to have the interest paid to you without tax being deducted. Your bank or building society will have the forms for you to complete that allow them to do this.

credit

Credit is a way of buying goods by delaying the payment, or by paying in instalments. The different types of credit include loans, credit cards and store cards.

Credit cards

Credit cards are very useful, but can cause difficulties if too much money is borrowed. They are normally not available to someone under 18. Like debit cards, credit cards allow people to buy goods and services from a huge range of shops and other suppliers, in person, over the phone or on the internet.

Credit cards enable the shop to be paid straightaway, but the customer is not billed until sometime later. This means that the customer is being lent the money to buy the goods by the firm issuing the credit card.

If you apply for a credit card, the firm issuing the card will check out your creditworthiness. A spending limit will be set on the account. A fee

will be charged if you go over this, and the card may be cancelled.

Each month you will receive a statement, showing how much you have spent, how much is owed, and the minimum payment that must be made. If you do not pay your bill in full, you will be charged interest. If you make no payment at all, you will be charged a further penalty.

You can compare the costs of different cards by looking at the Annual Percentage Rate (APR), which is the rate of interest charged by the firm issuing the credit card; the lower the APR, the lower the cost of borrowing.

Some types of borrowing on a credit card are more expensive than others. Using your credit card to withdraw cash can be more expensive than using it to buy goods.

Store cards These cards offer you credit when you buy goods at a particular store. You are sent a regular statement showing how much you have spent, and what you owe. You can pay a fixed minimum amount each time, with the rest being carried forward and appearing on your next statement. Interest is charged on the amount you haven't paid off. These charges are often higher than other types of credit card. You can check the store card's APR and compare it to your credit card.

borrowing

Borrowing from a bank or building society A bank or building society lends money either through allowing an overdraft or by making a loan.

Overdrafts A person becomes overdrawn when they spend more money than they have in their bank account. If you need to go overdrawn, you can usually arrange with your bank an authorised overdraft up to an agreed amount. Interest may be charged. The most expensive overdraft is an unauthorised one – which is run up without the agreement of the bank. Interest is paid on the amount overdrawn, and charges are added on top.

If you ever find yourself in this situation, it is important to get in touch with the bank as soon as you can. Students may be offered interest-free overdrafts.

borrowing

LOANS

A loan is an arrangement with your bank – or other financial institution – under which you are lent a specific amount of money. You enter into a contract for the loan. This will be at an agreed rate of interest and for a set period of time, during which you repay the full loan. If you are under 18 it is very unlikely that you will be able to get a bank loan, as these kinds of contracts with 'minors' are not usually binding. All loans are different – always check the small print to see what you are signing up to.

Buying goods by instalments – credit or hire purchase

You can often buy more expensive goods (cars, computers, TVs) by instalment – that is, by paying only part of the price at the time of purchase, and paying the rest later.

Sometimes credit is available interest-free, but credit is normally an expensive way of paying for things. It is always a good idea to check the charges (the APR) that are being made.

'Hire purchase' is a special form of buying on credit. Technically the shop sells the goods to a finance company and you pay to 'hire' them over an agreed period. When you have paid off what you owe, you make a final payment to purchase the goods (hence 'hire purchase'). Only then do you become the owner.

Second thoughts

If you signed a credit deal at home (or away from the shop or business premises) you have a right to cancel if you act quickly. You will be sent a second copy of the agreement that will tell you how to cancel if you want to. You will have five days to do this.

getting into debt

People get into debt for all sorts of reasons. They may find they owe money to several different people and are tempted to borrow more to pay off some of these debts. This often becomes even more expensive.

You know it's getting serious when you start getting badgered to make repayments by the people you owe money to – your 'creditors' – and you can't meet all the demands.

What to do

- **Don't ignore the problem:** it won't go away and will get worse the longer you leave it. You can get free help from a range of advice agencies.
- **Draw up a budget:** list all the money you owe and the people to whom it is owed; what your income and reasonable living expenses are; and see how much you can afford to pay back.
- **List your debts in their order of priority:** at the top are those where non-payment can have really serious consequences – like losing your flat or home; having the electricity or gas cut off, or where non-payment is a criminal offence (like council tax and your TV licence). You should aim to pay these off first and then work out what's left over for the others, treating them equally.
- **Contact all your creditors:** go and see them or write or phone; explain the position and show them your budget. Discuss with them what you can reasonably pay. Usually they will be prepared to negotiate. You may be able to agree to pay by instalments or, for a period of time, just to pay off the interest on your loan. If you are worried about contacting them directly you can contact a free advice agency for help.
- **Don't borrow more without getting advice:** some individuals or companies lend money at very high rates of interest, making it difficult to keep up with repayments and hard to get out of debt.

HELP

You can get help and advice from experts. Try the National Debtline or a Citizens Advice Bureau, see contacts.

insurance

Insurance is a way of protecting yourself and your property from an unexpected loss or mishap. You can insure yourself against almost anything – losing your possessions in a fire, having them stolen or damaged, or having to face unexpected medical bills on a holiday abroad. If you drive a car or motorcycle, you must be insured by law, (see travel, page 103).

In return for a premium – an agreed amount of money you pay each month or year – an insurance company will, if the worst does happen, pay you compensation for the losses or damage that you are insured against.

Buying insurance

There are two ways of obtaining insurance. You can either deal directly with the company, or go to a broker.

Most large insurance companies have offices in the major towns and cities. Their numbers are in the Yellow Pages or local phone book. You can often deal directly with them and arrange your insurance cover by phone, or on the internet. Insurance brokers are agents who can help you choose an insurer and arrange the policy for you. They don't usually charge you for this, but instead make their money from the insurance company that you have decided to use.

All the information you give should be accurate. Questions must be answered truthfully, and all other relevant information should also be given. If it's not, the insurance policy will be invalid and the insurer may refuse to pay your claim.

Keep a copy of any form that you complete, and when you renew your insurance (usually done each year) don't forget to tell the insurance company about anything that has changed that might affect your insurance position. If you don't, your policy may be invalid. Always check the small print to ensure that you get what you need included in your insurance.

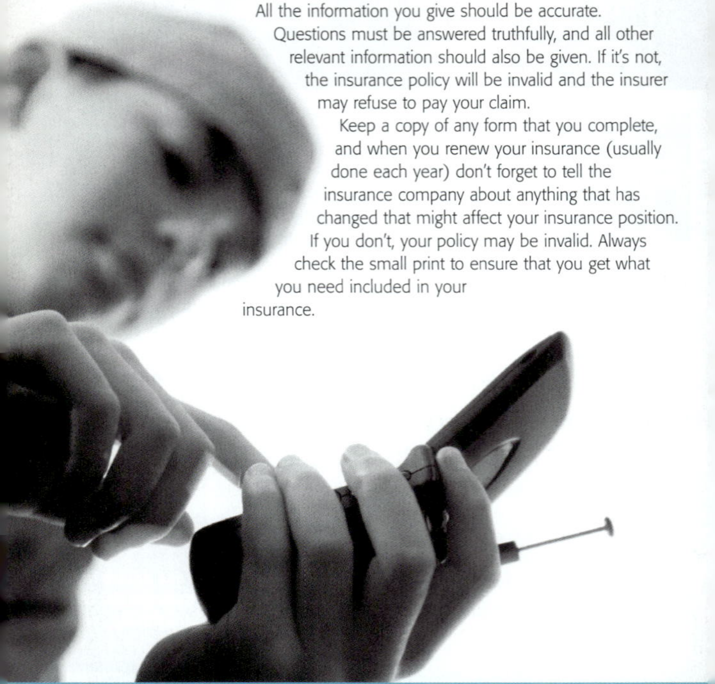

THE WORDS THEY USE:

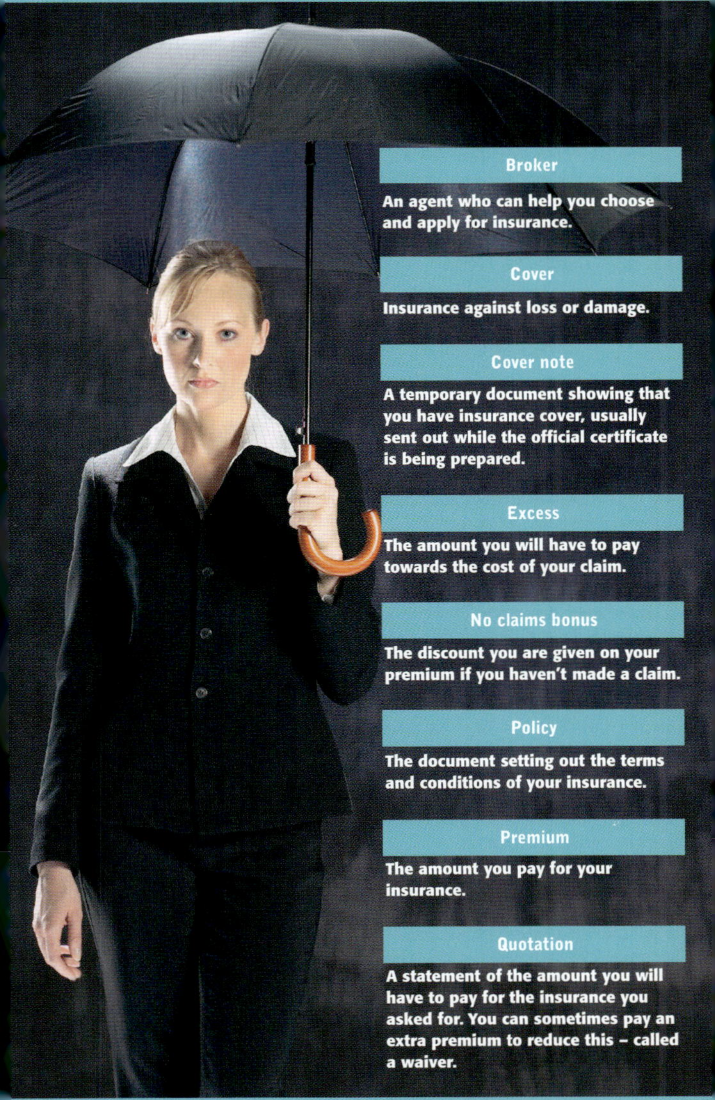

Broker

An agent who can help you choose and apply for insurance.

Cover

Insurance against loss or damage.

Cover note

A temporary document showing that you have insurance cover, usually sent out while the official certificate is being prepared.

Excess

The amount you will have to pay towards the cost of your claim.

No claims bonus

The discount you are given on your premium if you haven't made a claim.

Policy

The document setting out the terms and conditions of your insurance.

Premium

The amount you pay for your insurance.

Quotation

A statement of the amount you will have to pay for the insurance you asked for. You can sometimes pay an extra premium to reduce this – called a waiver.

tax

Income tax Money paid in income tax is used to pay for services provided by the state – such as health, education, defence etc. Everyone who earns or receives income over a certain amount in a year pays income tax and, generally speaking, the more you earn, the more you pay. Current tax rates on income range from 20%–40%. As well as earnings from full- and part-time work, tips and bonuses, tax is also paid on interest from savings with banks, building societies and some National Savings accounts. Income Support, profits from business and dividends from shares are also taxable.

PAYE (Pay As You Earn) Your employer will usually take the tax from your earnings each time you are paid and pass the money on to the tax authorities, called HM Revenue and Customs. Everyone is entitled to receive a certain amount of money on which they pay no tax at all. This is called a personal allowance, which, for a single person in 2008/2009, is £6,035. Income tax is paid only when your income rises above this. There are other allowances which may be available, e.g. for the cost of tools or special clothing if they are not provided by your employer. If you are on a training programme, your grant in most cases is not taxable.

Part-time workers should not have tax deducted from their pay, unless their income is above £116 a week. If you are a student with a holiday job, ask your employer for a form P38(S) if you think your total taxable income for the year (including earnings and income support), will be less than the basic personal allowance, i.e. £6,035. Fill in the form, return it to your employer, and you should then be paid without tax being deducted.

If you have been working and paying tax, but believe your total income for the year will be less than £6,035, ask for a P50 form from your local tax office, and return it completed with your P45 form from your employer. You should then receive a refund.

Failure to complete your tax forms correctly can mean extra interest payments and even fines. The HM Revenue and Customs runs a telephone helpline, giving information and advice on tax, see **contacts**. It also publishes free booklets on tax, obtainable from your library or nearest tax office under HM Revenue and Customs in the phone book.

Tax credits Working Tax Credits and Child Tax Credits are available to those on low incomes to top up earnings.

NATIONAL INSURANCE

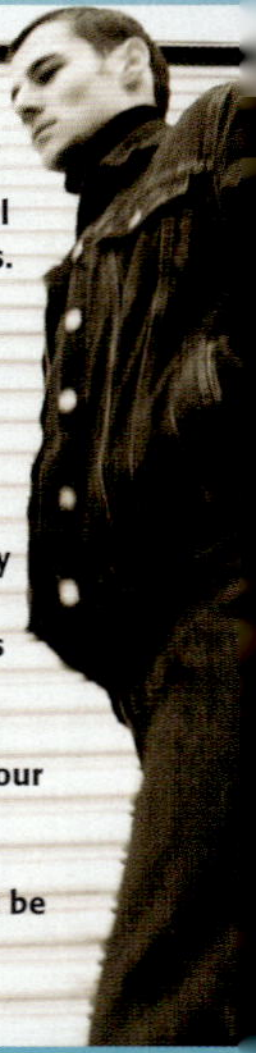

Almost everybody in Britain who is in paid work must pay National Insurance contributions. This money is used to help run the National Health Service and to provide benefits and pensions.

It is generally taken directly from the money that you earn by your employer. Everyone has their own NI number, which they receive just before they reach 16. Your NI number is used to record all your NI contributions and must be given when claiming benefits.

family

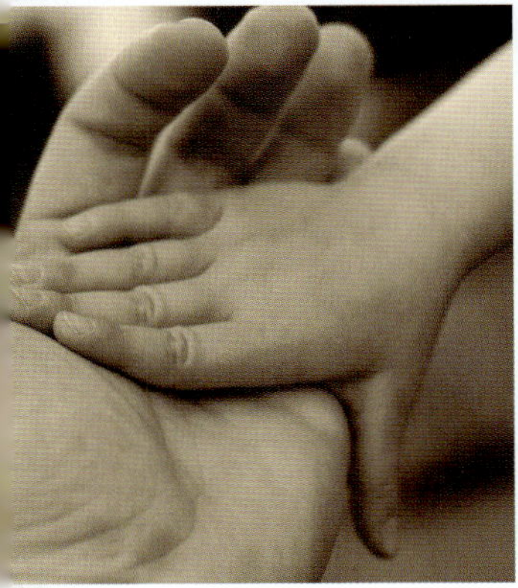

INDIVIDUALS ENGAGING IN SOCIETY

Citizenship Foundation

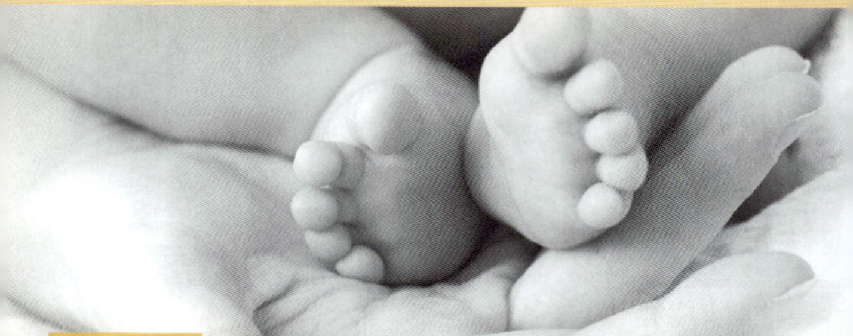

Registration

Within six weeks of birth, the birth and name of a child must be registered with the local registrar office. The birth should be registered in the district in which it took place. If this is not possible, the parent may visit a register office in another district, which will pass the details to the correct office.

The birth may be registered by either parent if they are married, but only by the mother if they are not. If unmarried parents want both their names to appear on their child's birth certificate, then they must both be present when the child is registered. The father's name can be registered later.

Changing your name

Under 18

A child's name can be changed with the agreement of both parents. If the child is in care or a ward of court, the child's name cannot be changed without the agreement of the court or everyone with responsibility for the child.

If a parent wants to change their child's name, but the other parent or the child objects – then that parent or the child can apply for a court order to prevent this. Courts are very reluctant to agree to change a child's name against their wishes because of the importance of a name to a child's sense of identity.

If you are under 16 and wish to change your name you will need your parents' agreement or a court order. If you are 16 or over you can change your name by deed poll and register it at court.

Over 18

You can call yourself what you like and, if you want to change your name, you can just go ahead and do it. You can't, however, change your name to mislead or defraud someone.

Although you are free to be known by whatever name you wish, it can be difficult to prove your identity if the name you use is not the same as the one on your birth certificate. The best way to confirm your new name is by a change of name deed poll. This is a legal document, signed by two witnesses, announcing a person's new name, witnessed by a solicitor. The Citizens Advice Bureau or a solicitor can give you more information on this.

If you marry

Women have the right to change their surname when they marry – but they don't have to. A woman can keep her own family name, or make a new one by joining her name with that of her husband. A new surname becomes official by signing the marriage register or a deed poll.

When he marries, a man may also take his wife's surname by using a deed poll.

citizenship

Most of our legal rights and responsibilities arise just because we are living, working or studying, in a particular place – in our case, Britain. This is citizenship in its widest sense.

Sometimes, however, people need to know which country they are legally connected to (or what their nationality is). Countries can base their rules on a number of questions, such as where the person was born, how long they have lived in the country and where their parents were born or live.

In brief

Anyone born in the United Kingdom before 1 January 1983 is automatically a British citizen. If you were born in the UK on or after this date, you are a British citizen by birth if either of your parents are British citizens, or they are entitled to live here permanently. If your parents are not married, only your mother's position counts - although if your parents married after your birth, you may still be entitled to citizenship.

Becoming a British citizen by naturalisation or registration depends on a number of different factors, such as if you marry a British citizen, how long you have lived here, if you are permanently settled here (or intend to remain here permanently) and if you are of 'good character' and speak sufficient English.

This is a complicated process and you will need specialist advice. Your local Citizens Advice Bureau can help you find this.

How the law works

There are no laws that list the exact rights and duties of parents. It is impossible to write down everything a parent should do for a child.

Instead, the law states that all married parents and unmarried mothers automatically have parental responsibility for their children. An unmarried father does not have automatic parental responsibility for his child. He can obtain parental responsibility by signing the birth register jointly with the mother, by agreement with her, by marrying her, or by registering for parental responsibility with the courts.

Parental responsibility This means having the responsibility and authority to care for the child's physical, moral, and emotional needs.

When a child or young person is taken into care, parental responsibility is given to the local authority, although parents do keep certain rights and responsibilities.

The law puts the interest of the child first. The powers that parents have to control their children are for the benefit of the child, not the parent. Those who deal with children in a legal setting, such as social workers, doctors and lawyers, must take careful note of what a child says, particularly when the child is able to understand all the issues involved. Parental responsibility ends when the child reaches 18, or as early as 16 if the child gets married. As a very experienced judge once said, 'in law, parents begin with a right of control, but by the time the child is 18 they can do no more than advise.'

Providing a home

Parents have a duty to look after and care for their children until they are 18. Once someone reaches the age of 18 they can normally leave home without their parents' permission. However, the police and other authorities are unlikely to stop anyone leaving home, even against their parents' wishes, unless they are under 16, in some kind of danger, or are unable to look after themselves. See **home**, page 81.

Discipline

Although corporal punishment is banned in schools and residential care homes, parents have the right and duty to discipline their child – and this can include smacking. But the corporal punishment must be 'moderate and reasonable'. If it is too harsh parents risk prosecution or having their child's name put on the child protection register, or the child being taken into care.

Education

Parents have a duty to make sure that their child has a suitable full-time education, between the ages of 5–16. See **education**, page 26.

Religion

Parents can decide the religion (if any) in which their child will be brought up. If they can't agree between themselves, they can go to court, where a judge will decide what is in the best interests of the child.

A court will listen to the views of the child concerned and these will be respected if the child clearly understands what is involved.

Medical treatment

In practice young people, aged 16 and over, can almost always agree to their own medical treatment without referring to their parents. However, in serious cases a court may overrule a child's refusal to consent to medical treatment. Before treating a young person under 16, however, a doctor will normally try to obtain the parents' permission unless it is an emergency or the young person is clearly able to understand what the treatment involves.

BABYSITTING

There is no law giving the minimum age for a babysitter, nor one stating how old a child must be before it can be left alone. Parents must take all the circumstances into account. For example, the age of the babysitter, the availability of the parent(s) or the health of the children being looked after, count as relevant factors.

Parents have a legal duty to care for their children, and even when the child is with a babysitter, the parent still has responsibility for their care and safety. This means that parents must choose a babysitter who is able to look after their children properly. If a serious accident occurs while they are out, the parents may have to convince a court that they had done all that they could to make sure their child was being looked after properly. A babysitter under 16 will probably be thought too young to deal with an emergency.

adoption

Anyone who is under 18, and has never been married, can be adopted.

A couple or an individual wishing to adopt a child must usually be at least 21. If a married couple wishes to adopt, and one partner is the father or mother of the child, the parent need only be 18, but the step-parent must be at least 21. Since 2005, unmarried couples – including gay and lesbian couples – can also adopt.

When children are adopted, they are treated in law almost as if they had been born to the couple or person who adopted them. Parents who adopt children are advised to be open about their child's birth family from the start.

At 18, people who have been adopted have the right to receive, from the adoption agency, any information that would help them obtain a copy of their original birth records. An interview with a counsellor to prepare them for this is available. For more information, see **contacts.**

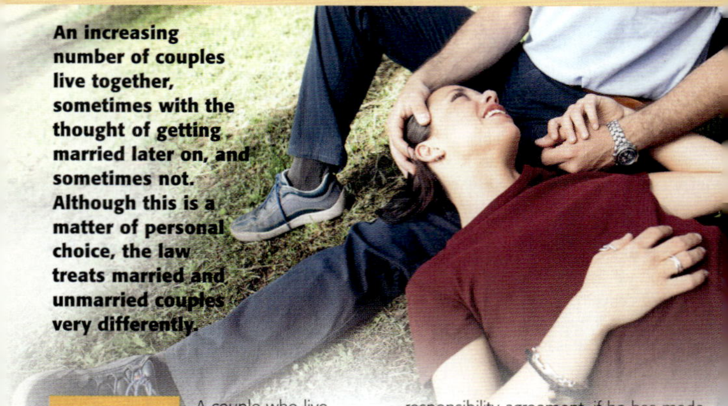

An increasing number of couples live together, sometimes with the thought of getting married later on, and sometimes not. Although this is a matter of personal choice, the law treats married and unmarried couples very differently.

Money and finance

A couple who live together without getting married are under no duty to look after one another, or to provide each other with financial support, unless it is something they have specifically agreed to do.

When children are involved, both parents, whether married or unmarried, have a legal responsibility to look after them and provide for them until they reach the age of 18.

If a married person dies without making a will, their wife or husband is entitled to all or most of their possessions. But if they were not married, and no will is present, it can be very difficult for the partner to obtain any of the deceased's possessions.

Children

Both parents, whether married or unmarried, are legally required to support and maintain their children.

Parents, who are married, automatically share parental responsibility (see page 72) for their children and can both take decisions about their children's upbringing. An unmarried father has this right only if the couple have signed a parental responsibility agreement, if he has made a successful application to court for parental responsibility or if his name is on his child's birth certificate.

Home

Married couples generally have equal rights to occupy their home, whether they rent or own it. This continues even if their marriage fails, unless the court orders otherwise.

Unmarried couples do not have this right. If the home is in just one person's name, the non-owner may not have any right to occupy the property. However, non-owners can obtain rights over the house if they make mortgage payments or help generally to improve or maintain the house. Couples can avoid difficulties caused by this by using a solicitor to write a formal contract setting out what would happen to their house and contents etc, should the relationship come to an end.

Breaking up

Unlike a married couple, people who live together can end their relationship anytime they choose, without having to go to court.

Getting married

Legally, no one can be forced to marry against their wishes, and each partner must be 16 or over and unmarried. A person who wants to marry, but is aged 16 to 18, needs their parents' written consent. It's a criminal offence if a couple gets married without this, but the marriage is still valid. However, marriages involving someone aged 15 or under, or members of the same sex (even after a sex change operation), are not recognised in law. Courts can issue an order to protect a person from being forced into marriage. If the order is broken, the offender can face two years in jail.

Almost anyone can be married in an Anglican church (unless they are divorced and their former partner is still alive). They need not be a churchgoer, but must satisfy the legal requirements and have a specific connection with the parish, such being a resident (either now or in the past), or having been baptised there. Members of other faiths must, before the religious ceremony, obtain a civil certificate or licence from the registrar in the district where they live.

Under the *Marriage Acts*, couples can choose to marry in any registry office in England and Wales or in other places that have been registered for marriages (such as a hotel or stately home).

Being married to more than one person at the same time – called bigamy – is normally a crime. But the marriages are recognised in England and Wales if they took place in a country that allows marriages of this kind, if each partner was legally free to marry in that way and not living in the UK.

Engagement

Until 1970 an engagement was seen as a legal contract. If someone breaks off their engagement today there is usually not even a duty to return the engagement ring. The ring is seen as a gift, and may be kept, unless it was originally agreed to return it if the marriage did not take place.

Civil partnerships

The *Civil Partnership Act 2004* allows same-sex couples, aged 16 and over, to register their partnership in a similar way to a civil marriage, and gives same-sex couples the same legal rights as people who marry. It means that, for the first time, same-sex couples have the same rights to property, benefits, inheritance and parental responsibility as those who are married.

The ceremony can take place in a registry office (or other licensed premises) – but not in a church.

If either or both partners wish to end the partnership, a formal court process takes place, through which the partnership becomes dissolved.

VIOLENCE

A court can make an order, called an injunction, to protect a victim of domestic violence and can order one partner to leave the home for the other's protection – even if they are married. It is important for anyone in this situation to get advice from a solicitor as soon as possible.

divorce

A couple, that longer wishes to live together, can either end their marriage by divorce, or separate, keeping the marriage legally alive. A separation may simply mean living apart, or it can be made more formal through what is known as a judicial separation.

When one or both partners decide to divorce, an application is made to the local county court or, in London, the Divorce Registry. It is usually made through a solicitor, but can be done by one of the partners alone (but not until at least one year after the date of marriage).

If both partners can agree over their finances and together make satisfactory plans for the care of their children, it will probably not be necessary for either to appear in court. Nor will there be any publicity in the papers. There are thousands of divorces each year, and the press cannot report the case unless the divorce is contested or reporting restrictions are lifted.

When the judge is satisfied that the appropriate arrangements have been made, that all the information is correct and that the marriage has broken down and cannot be saved, he or she will grant a decree nisi. Six weeks later, the person seeking the divorce can apply for a decree absolute. When this is granted, the marriage comes to an end.

Grounds for divorce

A person who applies for a divorce must prove to the court that their marriage has irretrievably broken down and that one of the following five things has happened…

1. The other partner has committed adultery, i.e. had sexual intercourse with another man or woman and it is intolerable to live together.
2. The other partner has behaved unreasonably. This covers many things, including assault, refusing to have children, being excessively dirty or anti-social.
3. They have lived apart for two years, and they both want a divorce.
4. They have lived apart for five years and only one partner wants a divorce.
5. One partner has deserted the other for at least two years immediately before the application.

Children

Parents going through a divorce are encouraged to reach an agreement between themselves over where their children will live and how often they will see each parent. But the judge will accept these arrangements only if satisfied that they are in the best interests of the child. If the child is felt to be old enough to have a view of their own, the judge will talk to them in private.

Parents who cannot agree over this are often advised not to go straight to court (expensive and stressful for all concerned), but to use independent counsellors to help them sort out these arrangements first. A court will, however, have to approve the final arrangements over children and money. It's usually felt to be in the children's interest to keep in touch with their family, so a judge will rarely stop a parent from seeing a child.

After the divorce, both parents normally keep parental responsibility for their child, and both should consult each other over decisions that affect their child's life, such as education, medical treatment, and religious upbringing.

Step-parents

Step-parents do not have parental responsibility for their stepchildren, but the courts can require them to support a stepchild. With their new partner, the step-parent may help with day-to-day things affecting the child, but major decisions should be taken by the child's birth mother and father – or only the mother, if they were not married (unless the father has parental responsibility). To change this, a step-parent may apply for parental responsibility or, together with the birthparent, adopt the child. See **contacts** for organisations able to give more information about this. If their relationship with the natural parent breaks down, the step-parent will have no rights over the child.

Grandparents

When a marriage ends, it may mean that a child is prevented from seeing other family members, such as grandparents, adding to the child's loss. In this situation, grandparents can apply to a court for permission to carry on seeing the child or to have the child stay with them – although this is more difficult to obtain than for parents.

Family disputes

Sometimes parents become involved in legal disputes which directly affect their children – especially if they are getting divorced and cannot agree who the children should live with. In really important cases a young person who shows enough understanding of the issues can act on their own initiative to instruct a solicitor and even make an application to the court. It is usually much better if their views can be reflected through a counsellor or mediator, as the whole process can be very stressful and damaging to relationships with parents or other family members. It is important to get specialist advice, see **contacts**.

young citizen's passport

home

INDIVIDUALS ENGAGING IN SOCIETY

Citizenship Foundation

Where do I look?

Advertisements for accommodation are found on the internet, in local newspapers, supermarkets and the student union, if you are at college. The local council housing department can tell you whether you are likely to qualify for council housing and can also give you details of local housing associations.

You can also try estate agents and accommodation agencies. These agencies are not allowed, by law, to charge you for information about housing or lists of vacancies. Don't agree to pay them a fee. Normally they are paid for their services by the landlord. If you are asked for money and have any doubts, check first with the local Citizens Advice Bureau or Shelter, see **contacts**.

You can't get a mortgage or buy a house until you are 18 and it can be difficult to rent somewhere if you're under 18 – unless you can find someone to guarantee the tenancy on your behalf until you are 18.

QUESTIONS TO ASK

What's the rent?

What does it include – council tax, electricity, etc? How often is it paid, and who is it paid to? Is any rent payable in advance? Rent paid in advance will be lost if you leave without giving the right amount of notice.

Your rent is fixed at whatever rate you agree with your landlord. If you think the rent demanded is too high you can ask the local rent assessment committee to decide what is reasonable for the property (ring your local council or look under 'rent officer' in the phone book). If you are an assured shorthold tenant (most are), you must do this within the first six months of the tenancy. There is no charge for this but the committee can only assess your rent if there are enough similar flats or houses being let in the area.

The rate fixed by the rent assessment committee applies for at least 12 months from the date the rent was fixed, and a tenant can make only one application to the

HOUSING BENEFIT

If you are on a training programme or Income Support, entitled to income-based Jobseeker's Allowance or have a low wage, you may qualify for Housing Benefit from your local council. Your local housing advice centre or Citizens Advice Bureau can help you work out what you're entitled to. Housing Benefit is not available to full-time students, unless they have children, a disability or are under 19 and are studying at school or college, i.e. not in higher education.

Discrimination

A landlord must not discriminate against a would-be tenant on grounds of race, religion or sex, unless the property is being shared with others, and the landlord (or close relatives) live at the property. It is also against the law for someone who sells or lets property to discriminate against a disabled person. Landlords and members of their immediate family who let out rooms to fewer than seven people in their own homes are not affected.

committee. It's a good idea to take advice before you do this, as your landlord may try to evict you. Sometimes the committee can put the rent up as well as down.

Do I pay a deposit? This is an amount (often equal to a month's rent) paid to the landlord or the agent at the start of the tenancy. Always ask for a receipt when you hand over your deposit.

If you cause damage or leave bills or rent unpaid, the landlord can take what you owe from your deposit. Try to agree any deductions with the landlord before you leave, otherwise you may find you've lost more of your deposit than you should.

What happens to my deposit?

Since 6 April 2007, your deposit must be held in a tenancy deposit scheme. This is designed to help tenants get back all or part of the deposit they are due when they leave the property, and also encourages landlords and tenants to make a clear agreement from the start about the condition of the property. Your landlord must give you details of the deposit scheme within 14 days of you paying the deposit, see **contacts**.

Do I need references? If so, choose people who have known you for a reasonable length of time but preferably not a close relative. It is important to ask the person concerned first.

How safe? Check the fire escape, plumbing, electrical fittings and heating appliances. Landlords must, by law, have all gas appliances checked each year and must get a certificate of safety that you are entitled to see.

Leaving home

Young people under 18 are still, in law, in the 'custody and care' of their parents, which means that, strictly speaking, they need their parents' permission to leave home. But, in reality, courts are unlikely to order anyone aged 16 or 17 who leaves home against their parents' wishes to return home unless they appear to be in some kind of danger or unable to look after themselves. See also **family**, page 72.

If you are 16 or 17 and homeless, or feel that you can no longer live at home because you are being hurt, or because life at home is so bad, you can get help from social services. Under the *Children Act 1989*, local authorities must provide accommodation for 16 and 17 year olds who are in need or whose welfare would be endangered if accommodation were not provided. However, some local authorities find it difficult to get hold of suitable accommodation for young people, and Income Support is not available to all 16- or 17-year-olds. Therefore, if you can, get advice from a housing advice centre, Citizens Advice Bureau, or your local council before you do anything.

In care If you are leaving care, your local social services have a legal duty to provide help and advice.

When you rent a flat or house, you normally sign an agreement with the landlord or their agent. This is known in law as a tenancy agreement, sometimes called a lease.

It should contain all the conditions agreed between you and the landlord, along with a list (called an inventory) of the furniture and other equipment that comes with the property. Make sure everything is included, and make a note (or ideally take a photograph) of anything that's damaged when you take up the property.

Read all documents carefully. Don't be afraid to seek advice from the Citizens Advice Bureau, a housing advice centre or a solicitor if parts are not clear, or if they contain conditions which you didn't expect. Don't sign until you fully understand the agreement and are prepared to accept what it says.

Normally you and the landlord will each sign, exchange and keep a copy of the tenancy agreement. Look after this. If there's any kind of problem while you're in the property, you'll need it to check your rights and duties.

Assured shorthold tenancy

This is the name given to the kind of tenancy that you will probably have if you rent a house or a flat. In fact, if your tenancy agreement was made on or after 28 February 1997, it must be of this type, unless you have some kind of written statement from the landlord saying it is not.

Your tenancy agreement will probably work like this:

- **You are assured of the right to stay as a tenant for the period stated in the agreement, unless you break the agreement in some way, in which case the landlord can apply to a court to get you to leave earlier. Assured shorthold tenancies used to be for a period of at least six months. This minimum period no longer applies.**
- **You can't leave before the date stated in the agreement, without being required to pay the balance of the rent, unless your tenancy agreement has a 'break clause' allowing you to leave early by serving an agreed period of notice, such as one month. You can ask for this to be included in your agreement.**
- **If you do not have a written tenancy agreement, and your tenancy is for a period of more than three years, you have a right to receive from your landlord a written statement of the terms of your tenancy. This includes the date that the tenancy began, the date that it ends, the amount of rent payable and the date that rent is due. The landlord can be prosecuted and fined if this**

information is not provided within 28 days of your request.

- The landlord must normally give you at least two months' notice to leave. With a six-month tenancy this will normally be at the end of the fourth month.
- If the landlord delays this and does not serve notice until the fifth or sixth month, or even later, you have the right (assuming you continue to pay the rent) to stay in the property for a further two months.
- If you stay on without the landlord's permission after the two months' notice has expired, the landlord is entitled to apply to a court for an order to have you evicted. This will almost certainly be granted, and you will then be expected to pay the costs of the court order as well as the rent for the extra time in the property. It is illegal for a landlord to evict you without a court order (see eviction, page 84).
- If you take on an assured shorthold tenancy you are legally responsible for the rent up to the end of the agreed period. If you are sharing the flat or house with someone and they leave, then their share of the rent must still be paid until a replacement is found.

Lodgings and hostels

You do not have the same rights if you are in lodgings or if your landlord lives with you in the same house and shares the basic services with you. Your landlady or landlord only needs to give you 'reasonable notice' (this can be seven days) and does not need to apply to a court to have you evicted.

If you are in hostel accommodation with a local council or housing association, they will not generally need a court order to evict you. They can give you notice at any time, as long as they keep to the terms of the tenancy agreement.

Council tenants

You have certain rights as a council tenant, which include staying in your house for as long as you want (assuming you pay your rent and do what your tenancy agreement says), taking in lodgers and being consulted about the running of the estate. The council has a right to take action against tenants who cause a nuisance to others on the estate. In serious cases this has led to tenants losing their homes.

tenancy agreements

Repairs and maintenance

Who is responsible? If your tenancy agreement is for less than seven years, as it almost certainly will be, your landlord is responsible by law for looking after the structure of the building, including outside fittings (such as gutters) and essential services (heating appliances – not cookers – sinks, baths and toilets and the water, gas and electricity supplies). Responsibility for other repairs depends on what is said in the tenancy agreement. Tenants are normally responsible for repairs for damage that they cause, but not for fair 'wear and tear'.

Getting them done Tell the landlord when the repairs need doing – and keep paying the rent. If the landlord does nothing and the problem concerns serious questions of health and safety, you can get in touch with the local environmental health office. They have the powers to get something done, and can make the landlord carry out the necessary work. Their number is in the phone book under the name of your local council.

If the problem is not serious, or the local council won't take action, check again that responsibility for the work lies with your landlord. If it does, write to the landlord explaining that you intend to undertake the work yourself and send at least three estimates of the cost. An example letter is provided above. Give your landlord at least two weeks to consider these. If, at the end of this period, there is still no sign that the repairs will be carried out, you may go ahead with them yourself, taking the cost from your rent. Keep detailed records of everything you've done and a copy of every letter you write and receive. If you are in any doubt, at any stage, seek advice.

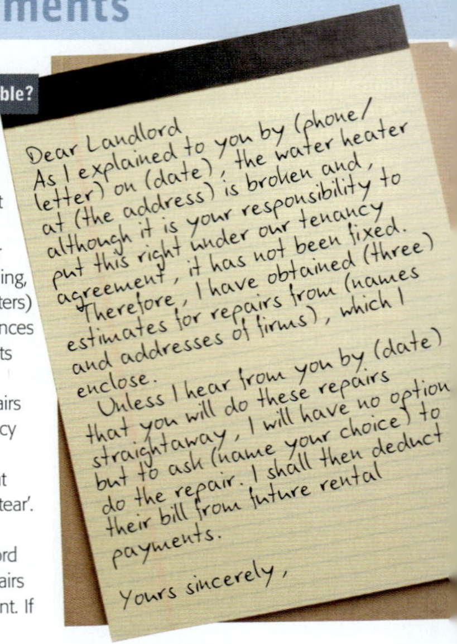

Dear Landlord

As I explained to you by (phone/letter) on (date), the water heater at (the address) is broken and, although it is your responsibility to put this right under our tenancy agreement, it has not been fixed.

Therefore, I have obtained (three) estimates for repairs from (names and addresses of firms), which I enclose.

Unless I hear from you by (date) that you will do these repairs straightaway, I will have no option but to ask (name your choice) to do the repair. I shall then deduct their bill from future rental payments.

Yours sincerely,

Eviction

Generally speaking, you cannot be made to leave the house or flat that you are renting, unless the landlord has given you notice in the correct way and obtained a possession order from a court. In most cases, it is a criminal offence for anyone to evict you without a court order or to try to force you out with threats. Court orders are not necessary, however, if you live in lodgings or your landlord lives on the premises. But your landlord still can't use violence to force you to leave. This is an offence under the *Criminal Law Act 1977*.

If you're threatened with eviction, get advice straightaway from a solicitor, your local council housing department or the Citizens' Advice Bureau. Make sure you keep on paying the rent. Failure to pay will make it easier for the landlord to require you to leave.

Harassment If your landlord stops short of physical violence but still behaves in a way designed to make you leave – like changing the locks, shouting abuse or playing loud music – they will be breaking the *Protection from Eviction Act 1977*. Again, your local council, housing advice centre or Citizens Advice Bureau can help. If physical violence is used or threatened, call the police.

BRIEF CASE: Laurie

brief case

A few weeks after signing a six-month tenancy agreement for a bed-sit, Laurie was told to leave. His landlord had decided to sell the house and knew he would get more money for it with Laurie out of his room. The lock on Laurie's door was taken off, and the landlord threatened to tip his possessions into a black plastic bag. Without a job, Laurie spent more than two months sleeping in his car. With legal advice and using legal aid, he took his case to court. The judge decided Laurie had been illegally evicted and ordered the landlord to pay him £36,500 in compensation – the extra amount of money the landlord made by selling his house without a tenant.

Insurance If you are living in rented accommodation, insurance for the building is normally arranged by the owner, but it's worth checking exactly what this covers. Building insurance will not cover the cost of replacing your things if they are damaged or stolen. You can arrange to insure your belongings through an insurance company or a broker, see **money**, pages 66–67.

If you have anything valuable, like a camera, stereo or jewellery, you will need to list it separately on the insurance and find out exactly how much it costs to replace. The same applies to something like a bike that may be stolen or lost outside the home.

Some policies will give you the full replacement cost; others take into account wear and tear and pay you less. If you are under-insured it means that your belongings are insured for less than their real value. If the insurance company discovers this when you make a claim, the amount they pay out is likely to be reduced.

Noisy neighbours The best way to tackle a problem of noise or any other nuisance is to talk to the person concerned, if possible, before the situation gets out of hand. Sometimes this is easier and more effective if several people complain together. If this doesn't work, write a simple letter (keep a copy), and allow a reasonable time for your neighbour to respond.

If that fails, get in touch with your local council or environmental health department. They have powers to investigate and deal with the matter, under the *Environmental Protection Act 1990*. See also **leisure**, page 95.

homelessness

Council help If you are homeless, the council housing department should be able to help. It has a legal duty to give you advice and help towards finding somewhere to live, but this is not the same as offering you somewhere to stay. The council has to house you only if you are 16 or over and:

- **homeless; and**
- **in priority need; and**
- **have a connection with the local area; and**
- **have not made yourself intentionally homeless.**

You should qualify as a priority need if:

- **you're pregnant; or**
- **you have a child who depends on you; or**
- **you've had to leave your last home because someone was violent towards you; or**
- **you've lost your home through something like a fire or flood; or**
- **your age, health problems or disability make you vulnerable and unable to cope with being homeless.**

If you are 16, 17 or under 21 and were in care before you were 18, you will be treated as a priority need. If you have recently left care, you are entitled to suitable accommodation until you are 18. Seek advice from Shelter or other housing advice centres, see **contacts**.

Sleeping rough This is dangerous and places the person at risk of being assaulted. Without an address, it is harder to get a job and even benefit. Under the *Vagrancy Act 1824*, someone found sleeping rough or begging may be fined. Under new law people who sleep rough can be given an anti-social behaviour order and face prison if they continue to break the law.

SQUATTING

A squatter is someone who enters and occupies land, or any part of a building, without the owner's permission. Squatting is not a crime but squatters may commit an offence if they cause damage when getting into the property or once they are there, or by using gas or electricity without first making the proper arrangements.

If squatters leave a place empty, the owner can break in and take possession but commits an offence if force is used while the squatters are still inside. An owner or tenant who intends to move in immediately and use the property as a place of residence, may use reasonable force in getting a squatter to leave, but normally requires a written statement or certificate showing that the property is needed as a home. In this situation a squatter commits an offence in refusing to leave.

Squatters can also be evicted from a property through the issue of a possession order by a court. There are a number of different types of order but, in some circumstances, squatters may have only 24 hours to leave and may not return to the property within the next 12 months.

Advice is available for anyone considering squatting, see contacts.

leisure

INDIVIDUALS ENGAGING IN SOCIETY
Citizenship Foundation

Not as planned

If you spend an evening at a match or concert looking at nothing more than a roof support or girder, then you have a right to complain and ask for a refund.

In fact, under the *Price Indications (Resale of Tickets) Regulations 1994*, it is a criminal offence for anyone reselling tickets (who is not the holder or promoter of the event or acting on their behalf) not to tell you about the location of your seat and anything that might spoil your enjoyment of the event.

There is no simple law setting out people's rights in the event of a change to the advertised programme or the cancellation of a performance. Your legal position will depend on such things as advance publicity, information given when the ticket was sold, and the circumstances that forced a change of plan.

Although disgruntled spectators have been successful in taking promoters to court, legal action is not recommended for disappointment over a cancelled event. Some promoters will try to retain goodwill by offering tickets for another performance, or refunds. If they don't, it's worth explaining why you think their action is *unreasonable* – a key word in cases of this kind.

Pubs and off-licences

The licensing laws controlling the sale of drinks were introduced in the First World War, and it's only in the last few years that they have begun to change.

Under the *Licensing Act 2003*, under 16s can go into pubs (if the management allows it) but they must be accompanied by someone over 18. At 16 or over, you can consume beer, wine or cider if it is bought for you by someone aged 18 or over, but only to drink with a meal in the dining or restaurant area of a pub when accompanied by someone aged 18 or over.

Only when you're 18 can you buy alcohol or drink alcohol in a bar. Drinks with 0.5% or less of alcohol, such as some canned shandy and low alcohol beers, are treated as non-alcoholic. It is an offence to sell alcohol to anyone under 18 – unless it can be shown that the landlord did their best to check the person was 18 or over. It's also an offence for you to buy, or try to buy, alcohol if you are under 18, or to buy or try to buy it for someone under 18. The maximum fine for this is £5,000.

The measures of alcohol that you can be sold are legally controlled. A reasonable head forms part of a pint of beer unless the glass has a line measure. The prices of drinks and food should be displayed by law, and should be clearly visible from where the drinks are served.

REFUSING TO SERVE

Pubs and off-licences can refuse to serve anyone with drink who looks as if they've had enough already, otherwise they can be charged with 'permitting drunkenness' and fined. Licensees have the right to ban or refuse to serve anyone they choose – unless it is because of their sex, religion, ethnic group or disability.

Not in public If a young person under 18 is in a public place (e.g. the street), or a place they have entered illegally, and have been drinking, or are about to drink, a police officer can, under the *Confiscation of Alcohol (Young Persons) Act 1997*, require them to stop drinking and can take away the alcohol. Refusal may lead to arrest or a fine of up to £500.

The police can also take alcohol from someone over 18 who is in a public place if they believe it will be passed to under-age drinkers.

The police can ask for the name and address of anyone from whom they have taken alcohol, and it is an offence to refuse to give these details or to give a false name and address.

The *Criminal Justice and Police Act 2001* allows for the consumption of alcohol to be banned in public places and gives the police powers to stop people from drinking and hand over the alcohol. Under the *Violent Crime Reduction Act 2006*, anyone aged 16 and over can be given a banning order preventing them from going to certain places if the police believe that disruptive behaviour may take place.

Proof of age If you have trouble proving you are over 18, you can apply for a proof of age card, carrying your name, photograph, date of birth and signature. Cards are available from Validate UK and Citizencard, see **contacts**.

Eating out

Quality

Whether you're in an expensive restaurant or an ordinary takeaway you have the right to reject any food of a quality below the standard that you are reasonably entitled to expect. What is 'reasonable' depends on such things as the price charged, what the menu says, and basic standards. The laws applying to faulty goods or services also apply. See **money**, pages 54–55.

Complaints

It's advisable to complain as soon as you know there's a problem and before eating food you believe is unsatisfactory, so that the restaurant can do something about the situation. The more you are paying, the higher the standard you're entitled to expect.

If the quality of your meal is poor, you are entitled to make a reasonable deduction from the bill, but don't leave without paying. Explain to the manager why you are not satisfied, and leave your name and address. It is then up to the restaurant to take this up with you later on if they wish.

Price

All restaurants, pubs and cafés must, by law, clearly display the price of food and drink where it is served, so you can read it before you order or sit down at a table.

Service charge

A service charge may sometimes be added to the bill in a restaurant. It is usually around ten per cent. If it was made clear before you ordered that service will be included, then you have got to pay it. If the service was unsatisfactory, see the manager to ask for a discount. If there is no service charge included, it is up to you whether to leave a tip.

Safety

Under the *Food Safety Act 1990*, it is an offence for a restaurant to serve food that is unfit for human consumption. If you are concerned about the hygiene in a place where you have eaten, you can contact your local environmental health office, which has the power to investigate.

BRIEF CASE: Prosecuted

The owner of two takeaways in Leeds was sentenced to two months in prison for failing to bring his restaurants up to the required standards, despite three warnings by local environmental health officers. Problems found during a spot check included dirt and food debris on the floor, grease and mould around the taps, food in the fridge three months out of date, and a pan of cooked chicken left out at room temperature all day. Because of the court action, the owner was declared bankrupt and lost both premises.

Raves

Anyone who organises a rave needs an entertainment licence. To get one the event must meet certain safety standards. Many raves are legal and are arranged in conjunction with the local licensing authorities. Unlicensed raves are illegal.

Under the *Criminal Justice and Public Order Act 1994*, the police have the power to break up an unlicensed open air rave of more than 20 people if the noise and disturbance are likely to cause distress to local people. Under the direction of a senior police officer, the police can order off the land anyone who is preparing, waiting for, or attending the rave. They can also seize and confiscate any sound equipment. Anyone who goes back onto the land within seven days can be fined or imprisoned for up to three months. The police can also stop anyone within five miles of the rave, and order them not to proceed to the gathering. Anyone who refuses to turn back may be fined.

Although the police have the powers to close raves and unlicensed parties that break the law, some forces prefer not to get involved unless there is a danger to people's safety or a serious nuisance.

Drugs

Despite the drug culture that surrounds raves, the possession of drugs remains illegal and can lead to a criminal record, a fine and imprisonment. In addition, taking ecstasy causes a rise in body temperature. Coupled with the heat inside the building, there is a serious danger of dehydration or heatstroke if body fluid is not replaced. It's advisable to drink about a pint of water every hour and to take regular breaks. Alcohol doesn't help, as it dehydrates the body even further. For more information on drugs and the law, see **life**, page 10.

GAMBLING

It is illegal for anyone under 18 to enter or to gamble in a betting shop, casino, a bingo club or to take part in these activities over the internet. Anyone who invites or allows someone under 18 to gamble also commits an offence. Jackpot machines and higher pay-out cash machines are restricted to those aged 18 or over.

Pools, lottery tickets and scratch cards should not be sold to anyone under 16 and winnings cannot be collected by someone below this age.

Nightclubs

Nightclubs must have special licences for entertainment and the sale of alcohol. Like pubs, it's illegal to sell alcohol to someone under 18, and owners are within their rights to choose who they will or will not allow in, as long as they do not break the anti-discrimination laws. Clubs who charge lower entry fees for women than men are breaking the law.

The door

Bouncers have no special legal powers. The same laws apply to them as everyone else, which means that they can only use a reasonable amount of force to throw someone out. In certain circumstances this means no force at all – and a bouncer who uses too much force without good reason commits an offence.

Under the *Private Security Industry Act 2001*, all door supervisors must now be licensed and display their licence badge clearly when working. It is an offence for a supervisor or security guard to operate without one.

Black cabs, licensed taxis

These are under tight licensing control. The vehicles must be checked regularly, the fares are set by law and the drivers may have had to sit an exam to get their licence. Black cabs can be flagged down, as well as hired from a taxi rank. From a rank a taxi driver cannot unreasonably refuse to take a fare. It is a criminal offence for a driver of a cab to lengthen the journey in time or distance without a good reason.

Under the *Disability Discrimination (Transport Vehicles) Regulations 2005*, newly licensed taxis must be fully accessible to disabled travellers. Black cab and licensed taxi drivers are also required to help disabled people into and out of taxis and to help them with their luggage – unless they have an injury or medical condition that prevents them from heavy lifting.

Minicabs, private hire cars

All minicabs, private hire cars, and their drivers, must be licensed by the local authority. If you want a private hire car, you should either book it in advance or wait in the cab office. Even if there's a meter, it's a good idea to get an estimate of the fare before you set off. If there's not, always agree the fare in advance. Minicabs and private hire cars are generally unaffected by the *Disability Discrimination Act*.

Unlicensed taxis

Unlike black cabs or licensed taxis, these vehicles will not have been specially examined and may not even have a current MOT. They will not be insured to carry fare paying passengers, so passengers have little protection if anything goes wrong.

No entry

The driver of a licensed taxi or hire car who without good reason refuses to take a passenger (including a disabled person) may be prosecuted and fined under the *Town Police Clauses Act 1847*. Anyone who feels that they are a victim of this, and wishes to do something about it, should make a note of the plate or registration number of the taxi or hire vehicle and report it to their local licensing authority. (The main local council switchboard can provide the number.) The licensing authority will investigate the case and then prosecute the driver if they feel there is sufficient evidence.

Parties

Drink and drugs

Although you can't buy alcohol from an off-licence until you're 18, anyone over five can drink alcohol on private premises. It is an offence to give alcohol to a child under five, unless given by a doctor or in an emergency.

An offence is committed, under the *Misuse of Drugs Act 1971*, if you knowingly allow anyone into your flat or house to supply an illegal drug to someone else, or allow the smoking of cannabis or opium. The penalty for someone knowingly allowing their flat or house to be used for these purposes is up to 14 years in prison for a Class A or B or C drug. Even if you are not taking the drug yourself you can still be charged as it is your place they are using. For more on the law and drugs, see **life** pages 10–12.

Safety

You invite some friends around for the evening and one of them falls down the stairs. If the cause of the accident was the state of the carpet rather than too much beer, you or your parents could be liable for their injuries. This doesn't mean wrapping every sharp corner in cotton wool, but something like a loose piece of stair carpet definitely should be fixed, since it is reasonable for visitors to expect to walk down the stairs safely. You're not expected to guard against the unforeseeable. If someone slides down the banisters and breaks a leg, then that's their problem.

Insurance

If someone is injured in your home you could be required to pay them compensation – although this can be paid through an insurance policy, if you have one. Most householders' insurance policies cover owners for injuries to other people called 'third parties' caused by the state of the buildings or its fittings. If you're in rented accommodation, your landlord could be liable – and again it is his or her insurance company that would pay damages. If you face this problem you can check with a solicitor or Citizens Advice Bureau.

Gatecrashing

Gatecrashing is trespass. The law says that you can use reasonable force to get gatecrashers to leave, but don't start waving a broken bottle around. This is unreasonable and will leave you in more trouble than them. If they come in peacefully, they should be asked to leave before any force is used.

Noise If there is a noisy party and the police are called, they can ask people to be quiet, but there's not much else they can do unless they fear there's going to be a breach of the peace – that is some kind of disorder. Then arrests will almost certainly be made.

However, if you are being disturbed by noise from a neighbour between 11pm and 7am, you can ring the local environmental health department, which must investigate your complaint as soon as possible. Under the *Noise Act 1996*, they have the power to send an officer to the house to measure the noise and decide whether it is excessive. If it is, the person believed to be responsible will be given a warning notice, giving them at least 10 minutes to switch off or turn down the noise. An offence is committed if the noise continues; the officer can decide to prosecute or issue an on-the-spot fine of up to £100. If the fine is paid within 14 days no further legal action can be taken for the offence; if it is not paid, a court can impose a higher fine.

If the warning notice is ignored, the officer can also obtain a warrant (often very quickly) to go into the building and remove the sound equipment that is being used.

For other problems with noisy neighbours, see **home**, page 85.

TV, videos, music, games and the internet

TV licence

You need a TV licence if you use a TV or any other equipment to receive or record TV programmes (such as DVD or VCR, a set-top box or a PC with a video card). Failure to have a valid licence can result in a court appearance and a fine of up to £1,000.

One licence covers all the equipment in a single home. If rooms are rented separately, a licence must be obtained for the TV equipment in each room.

Students living away from home are generally not covered by their parent's licence, unless they are using a small pocket-sized TV, powered by internal batteries, or a laptop with a television card which is not plugged into the mains when in use. Students who live in a hall of residence and have a TV in their room need their own TV licence.

A person does not have to let a TV licensing enquiry officer into their home, unless they have a search warrant.

Taping and recording You can tape or record a TV or radio programme for your own use, but only to listen to at a more convenient time. Strictly speaking, it's against the law to record a programme just because you find it particularly enjoyable or to keep it as part of a collection.

Copying a CD, tape or computer game without permission from the copyright owner is also illegal.

The internet All music and recordings of music are copyrighted (that is owned by someone) – for at least 50 years from the date on which they were published or recorded.

Downloading music files (whether for personal use or for profit) without permission from the copyright owner (e.g. the artist or record label) is a breach of copyright and is illegal, unless it is done with permission from the record label. This is because the person responsible has obtained for free something that they would normally have to buy. (In recent years, the British record industry has taken legal action against a number of people accused of down- or uploading music.)

A small number of artists provide music for free or let you decide what to pay for tracks that you copy. Lists of legal digital music services are available from the industry's website, **www.bpi.co.uk**.

BRIEF CASE: Warning

In 2004, 350,000 messages were sent to computer users, warning that unauthorised file sharing is illegal. Legal action was taken against 28 people who, it is alleged had uploaded thousands of music files onto filesharing networks.

BRIEF CASE: No excuse

A mother of a 14-year-old girl faced a bill of £4,000 to be paid in compensation for the music files that her daughter had illegally downloaded on the family computer. The mother stated that she herself was not computer literate and had no idea what her daughter had been doing.

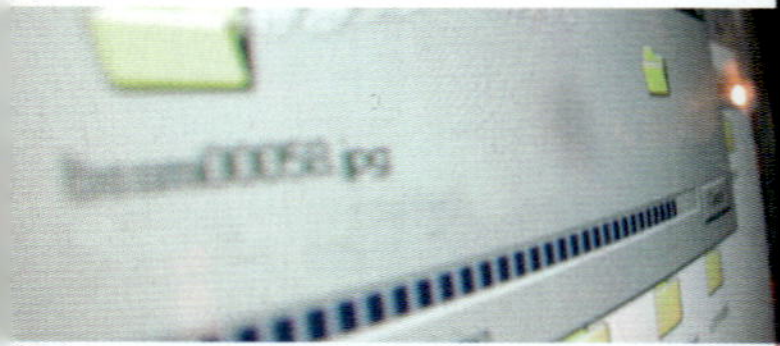

Pornography Accessing pornography, in general, is not an offence, unless it involves children (i.e. young people under 18). This is dealt with very strictly in law, and it is an offence to take, distribute, or possess an indecent photograph of a child.

The government is considering making it an offence to possess violent or abusive pornography, punishable by up to three years in prison. This means that it would become an offence for someone deliberately to view such material on a computer.

Safety

Under the *Sporting Events (Control of Alcohol etc) Act 1985*, it is an offence to be drunk at a football match or to have alcoholic drinks in the ground, or on certain coaches and trains travelling to or from the event. At the moment the law only applies to football.

Risks and the duty of care

Anyone who plays sport must expect a certain element of risk. But intentional or reckless behaviour towards someone else is a different matter, and the person responsible can be sued for damages and prosecuted for a criminal offence. Organisers of sporting events also have a duty to see that visitors, spectators and passers-by are reasonably safe.

BRIEF CASE: Football

A Stockport County player was awarded £250,000 after his career was ended through injuries suffered in a match against Swansea City. The court decided that he was brought down by a tackle aimed at the legs, rather than the ball, which did not reflect the reasonable care that players should show towards one another.

Banned

Under the *Football (Disorder) Act 2000*, a court can ban a person from attending domestic or international football matches where an offence is committed within 24 hours either side of kick-off or up to five days before an international fixture.

Walking

All land in the United Kingdom is owned by someone – private landowners, a local authority, government body (e.g. Ministry of Defence), or the Crown (the Queen). You will not usually end up in court by stepping on to a piece of land marked "trespassers will be prosecuted". Trespass is not usually a crime (unless you also cause damage) – it's a civil offence. A landowner can require the trespasser to leave, but in doing so may use only a reasonable amount of force. If the trespasser refuses to go, the landowner should call the police.

Footpaths If a route across a piece of land has been used for 20 years or more without interruption, that route becomes a right of way. A footpath cannot be lost through disuse. Once a right of way has been established it can be used forever unless it is closed by an order made under the *Highways Act 1980* or the *Town and Country Planning Act 1990*.

Strictly speaking, footpaths are for walkers only. It's a criminal offence to drive a motorbike or car on a path. Footpaths are shown on Ordnance Survey maps – but if you need to check on a path, you can ask to look at the maps in the local council planning office.

Under the *Rights of Way Act 1990*, when land is ploughed or any crop (except grass) is planted over a public footpath, the landowner must, within 14 days, make sure that the line of the path is clear to anyone using it. It is also an offence to put up a misleading sign, such as 'private' that discourages people from using a public right of way. If you come across a problem of this kind and want something done, contact the local council.

The local council's Rights of Way Officer has a duty to make sure that public rights of way are kept open and free from obstruction. It's the local council's responsibility to maintain footpaths so that people can walk along them, and the job of the landowner to look after stiles and gates along the path, footpath, or bridleway.

The *Countryside and Rights of Way Act 2000*, provides a 'right to roam' on land designated as open country. Landowners can impose restrictions on how the land is accessed or used (e.g. dogs to be on a lead). You can check with Countryside Access to see which land is open, see **contacts**.

BULLS

Checking your legal rights here needs some farming knowledge and the ability to tell one breed of bull from another without getting too close. All dairy bulls (breeds like Friesian, Guernsey and Jersey) are banned from fields crossed by public paths. Other types of bull are allowed only if they are in with cows or heifers, which apparently makes them much less aggressive.

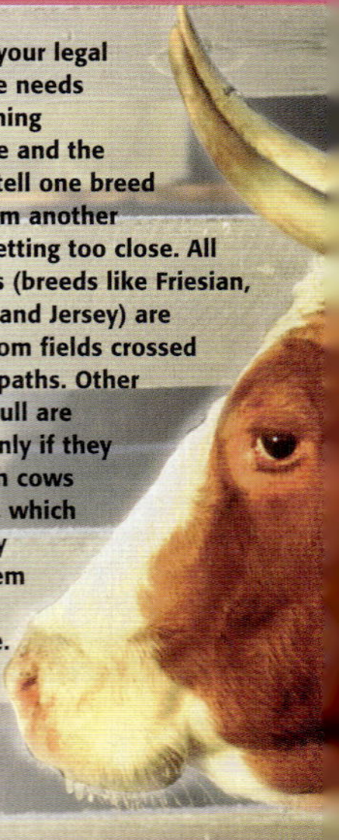

Rivers, canals and the sea

There is a public right to use a canoe or boat only on the tidal section of a river. Beyond this point you need permission from the owner of the riverbank to use the river. You also need a licence to use a boat or canoe on a canal – obtainable from British Waterways (the number of your local office will be in the phone book) and the British Canoe Union. Anyone is free to use a boat or to water-ski or jet-ski on the sea. However, if you want to jet-ski, water-ski or windsurf in a harbour you may require a licence and ferries and other shipping have a right of way.

Fishing

You can fish in the sea and in tidal waters at any time, unless there are local by-laws forbidding it. Fishing off a pier usually needs a licence. Anyone aged twelve or over who fishes for salmon, trout, freshwater fish or eels must have an Environment Agency Rod Fishing Licence, available from post offices or online from the Environment Agency website, see **contacts**. The licence covers England and Wales. Permission is also required from the landowner or the person owning the fishing rights.

Pollution

The Environment Agency asks members of the public to report any environmental incident – on rivers, lakes, canals or the coastline – or the dumping of rubbish, by ringing their local Environment Agency office (in the phone book) or by calling 0800 807 060, see **contacts**.

Beaches

Land between the low and high tide lines is the property of the Crown – but there is almost never a problem in walking along a beach. However, there is no right to get onto a beach over private land, unless there is a public right of way.

BRIEF CASE: Katrina

Katrina noticed that the water in Ackhurst Brook near Wigan, where she lived, was an unusual colour – particularly around the discharge pipe used by a local factory. She rang the Environment Agency who sent an officer to investigate. The officer reported that the water was discoloured and smelt foul and contained pieces of food that looked like shells from baked beans – which is just what they were. The company admitted polluting the river and was fined £5,000 by local magistrates.

animals

Wildlife

The *Wildlife and Countryside Act 1981* protects a wide range of wild animals, birds and plants and covers killing, injuring, taking or possessing, selling, and disturbing their place of shelter or protection. For an up-to-date list of protected species, see Whitaker's Almanack, available in most libraries and the RSPB website. *The Wild Mammals (Protection) Act 1996* makes it an offence to inflict unnecessary suffering on any wild mammal.

Pets

Under the *Animal Welfare Act 2006*, a young person is not allowed to buy a pet on their own until they reach the age of 16, nor can they, below this age, win an animal as a prize, unless they are accompanied by an adult.

It is also an offence to be cruel to an animal and to fail to look after all its welfare needs. The animal must be given a suitable place to live, a good diet and be protected from injury, pain and disease.

Under the *Animals Act 1971*, pet owners are also responsible for any damage their animal causes if they knew (or should have known) it was likely to cause such damage, or if their animal is defined as dangerous.

Dangerous animals are known, in law, as those that are not domesticated in this country and might be expected to have dangerous characteristics, such as a monkey or snake. Anyone keeping an animal of this kind must have a licence.

Dogs

Under the *Control of Dogs Order 1992*, anyone owning a dog must make sure that it wears a collar with the name and address of its owner when it is in a public place. If a dog fouls a footpath, the person in charge of the dog commits an offence if he or she fails to clear up the mess.

It is an offence under the *Dangerous Dogs Act 1991*, to allow a dog to be dangerously out of control in a public place. The owner, or person in charge, of the dog can be fined or imprisoned for up to six months. The court can also order the dog to be destroyed, and can disqualify the owner from keeping a dog in the future. A farmer is allowed to shoot a dog that is not under anyone's control and is worrying livestock on their land.

Under the *Guard Dogs Act 1975*, guard dogs should be under the control of a handler or else tied up and prevented from roaming freely. A warning notice should also be displayed. The Act does not apply to dogs guarding private houses or farmland.

BRIEF CASE: Lisa

When Lisa had to go away unexpectedly, she said that she asked a friend to feed and water her pet rat, Ziggy. After Lisa had been gone for six days, one of Lisa's neighbours told the RSPCA that the animal was in need of care. They found the rat with just a scrap of cheese and no water. It was dehydrated, trembling, and close to death. Lisa, who was unemployed, was fined £80 and told to pay £50 towards the cost of the case.

young citizen's **passport**

travel and transport

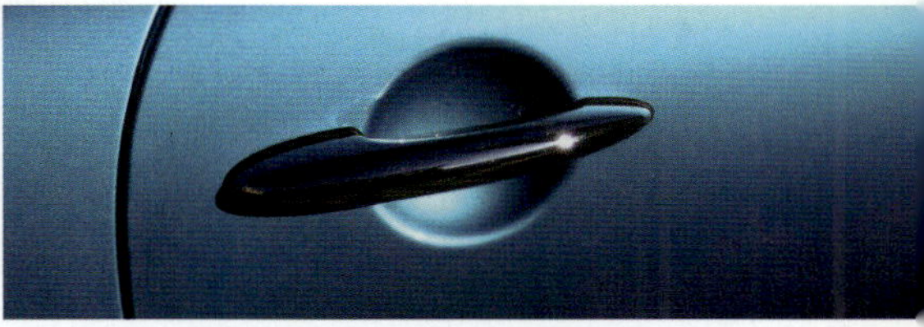

INDIVIDUALS ENGAGING IN SOCIETY

Citizenship Foundation

Package holidays

When you book a holiday, you are making a contract with the tour organiser – that is the company responsible for arranging the package. This is usually the tour operator, but it can also be the travel agent, particularly if you have asked for extra arrangements to be made, not included in the brochure.

Although holiday brochures are designed to show the hotel or resort at its best, the *Package Travel, Package Holidays and Package Tours Regulations 1992* state that they must be accurate and not misleading. If the room or the swimming pool that you were promised is not available, you may be able to claim compensation because of the failure of the company arranging the holiday to keep its side of the contract. It is also an offence, under the *Trade Descriptions Act 1968*, for a firm to make a statement that it knows to be false about the goods or services it provides. Prosecutions for this are usually made by local trading standards officers.

It's important to tell the travel agent or tour operator if you have any special needs at the time you make the booking.

Before you sign or hand over any money, read the small print to check what it says about changes to your schedule. Under certain circumstances, travel organisers can alter flight times or accommodation arrangements provided they make this clear in the brochure or contract. If you pay all or part of the cost of the holiday by credit card, you may be entitled to claim a full or partial refund from the credit card company if the firm organising the holiday fails to keep its side of the contract. For more information on paying by credit card, see **money** page 62–63.

If you go abroad, book through a travel company registered with ABTA, IATA or ATOL. If the travel firm belongs to one of these organisations, you'll find their symbol in the brochure. They will cover the cost of getting you home, or compensate you for your losses if the company you've booked with goes bust while you're away, or before you've left.

BEFORE YOU GO

- **Check whether you need to have any vaccinations, and think about getting medical insurance, (see below).**
- **If you are travelling in the European Union, or to Iceland, Liechtenstein, Norway or Switzerland get a European Health Insurance Card, allowing you free or reduced medical costs. Further information is available from post offices and the EHIC website, www.ehic.org.uk**
- **Check your passport is up to date and whether you need a visa for the country you are visiting. British citizens do not need to take a passport to travel to the Republic of Ireland, but some form of identification is required (photo ID, bank card, etc).**
- **If you're thinking of hitching, check before you go. In some countries it is illegal.**
- **If you need to know more about travel requirements or conditions, ring the embassy of the country concerned, or visit the 'Travel advice by country' section of the Foreign & Commonwealth Office website at www.fco.gov.uk or telephone their *Travel Advice line* on 0845 850 2829.**

TRAVEL AND MEDICAL INSURANCE

Travel insurance will protect you from losses while you're away and even illness before you go.

Take the policy with you on holiday, so that if anything goes wrong you can make sure you keep to the terms of the agreement.

Passports Everyone who travels abroad, including young children, must have their own passport. Passport interviews are now required for anybody aged 16 or over when applying for a passport for the first time.

A passport for someone aged 16 or older costs £72 and is valid for ten years, for travel to any country of the world. A passport for someone under 16 costs £46 and is valid for five years. See **contacts** for further details.

If something goes wrong If there is a problem with the holiday that the travel company has provided, tell them or their representative as soon as possible. If you're still not satisfied, make a note of the facts (photographic evidence may be helpful) and then contact the travel firm as soon as you get home.

If you're not satisfied with their reply, write to the managing director of the travel firm. If the company belongs to ABTA, you can have your claim decided by an independent person called an arbitrator (see **contacts**). If this is not possible, get advice from the Citizens Advice Bureau and, if necessary, a solicitor. Going to court is a last resort.

If your luggage doesn't arrive, report the loss immediately. Try to obtain a copy of any reports that you complete. Under international law, the airline is responsible for lost or damaged luggage, but compensation is paid by weight rather than value, and the airline will not be responsible for fragile items. It may be better to claim through your holiday insurance.

Lost or stolen If you lose all your cash or cards, you can go to a bank and arrange for money to be transferred from home. There will probably be a charge, but it should arrive within 24 hours. Immediately report the loss of traveller's cheques or credit cards to the company offices.

If you lose anything valuable, tell the police and get a note from them confirming that you have done this. Contact the travel company if you lose your ticket home. They often let you reverse the charges for the call. It is very important to report losses to your insurance company within the time limit stated in the policy.

If your passport is lost or stolen, contact the British Consulate who have an office in most big cities and should be able to provide you with help or advice.

In trouble Travellers overseas are automatically subject to the laws of the country they are visiting.

If you're arrested insist on the British Consulate being informed. The Consulate will explain the local procedures, including access to a lawyer and the availability of legal aid. A European Union (EU) national can go to any EU Consulate. See **the European Union** page 145.

DELAYS

If you are on a flight to or from an airport in the EU, which is delayed or cancelled, you may be entitled to free assistance, depending on the length of your flight and the period of delay. If you are delayed for more than two hours, you are entitled to free meals and refreshments and to make up to two free telephone calls, emails, telexes or faxes. Passengers delayed for more than five hours are entitled to a refund, if they decide not to travel, and to free hotel accommodation and transport, if delayed overnight. These rules apply to all flights from EU airports and to all incoming flights on EU airlines.

holidays

Taking a car or motorcycle

You'll normally need to get a Green Card from your insurance company, which extends your motor insurance to countries other than Great Britain. (This is not strictly necessary in EU countries, although it is advisable to take either a Green Card or your certificate of insurance.)

It is also worth checking with a motoring organisation, who will advise you whether you need an International Driving Permit (AA, RAC and Green Flag will tell you if you need an IDP and can issue one, if required).

If you have an accident, tell the police and ask for a record or receipt. It will help with your insurance claim when you get home. For the same reason, it's also a good idea to take notes and photographs of the incident, including pictures of the number plates of the vehicles involved.

Don't sign anything in a language that you don't understand. If you're put under pressure, write 'I don't understand' immediately above your signature.

Coming home

If you are returning from a country within the EU, you do not have to pay customs charges on any goods you bought in that country, and there is generally no limit on the amount you can bring in – as long as the goods are for a gift or your own use.

Limits are, however, placed on alcohol and tobacco and anyone who exceeds these must convince the customs that the goods were not bought for commercial purpose, that is to be sold on. Limits on tobacco brought from some EU states in Eastern Europe are lower than elsewhere. No one under 17 is entitled to a tobacco or alcohol allowance.

Customs officials can check your baggage for prohibited goods or to see if you need to pay any tax or duty if you have been to a country outside the EU. Details of the powers and duties of customs officers are given in the Travellers' Charter, available from HM Revenue and Customs website, see **contacts**.

getting about

Buses and trains

Tickets

By the time you're 16, you generally have to pay full fare on all buses and trains, trams and the Underground. In some areas full fare is charged on buses from the age of 14.

If you travel on a train or the London Underground without a ticket, you may be charged with an on-the-spot penalty, as well as the cost of your fare. Information about this is displayed in stations where this system is in operation.

If you are stranded at a station without any money for a ticket, your ticket can be bought for you by someone else at another station, with the authorisation sent by telephone to where you are waiting. This is known as a silk arrangement.

Some tickets are cheaper when travelling outside the rush hour, and travel cards give you further reductions.

- A 16-25 Railcard costs £24 for one year or £65 for three years (2009) and entitles you to a third off some ticket prices. Everyone aged 16-25 is eligible to have one, as are full-time students aged 26 and over. You can buy the Railcard at main stations, some travel agents, from student services at college, by phone or online, (see **contacts**).
- An Inter-Rail Pass lets you travel by train at a reduced rate in one or more European country, with discounts available on ferries. You must be a citizen of (or have lived in) a European country for at least six months and have a passport. See **contacts** for further details.
- The Young Person's Coachcard entitles young people aged 16-26 to up to a 30% discount on UK coach journeys. A one-year card costs £10, and £25 buys a card valid for three years.
- The Under 26 International Youth Card and the Euro<26 card provide members with discounted air fares worldwide, and also offer reductions on places to stay and visit (see **contacts**).

COMPLAINTS

If your train (or bus) is late, there's not a lot in law that you can do about it. When you buy a ticket, you have no legal guarantee that the train will run on time (or even at all), or that you'll have a seat when it does come. All this is explained in the small print, known as the conditions of carriage, which can be checked at station ticket offices.

Under the rail company's Passengers' Charter you may be offered a percentage of the ticket price in compensation if you're stuck on a train that has been seriously delayed, for one hour or more, or if you have a season ticket for a train service that has been below the standard set for punctuality or reliability.

Complaints about a train service can usually be made on each rail company's website, or on a complaint form available from a station on the route that you travelled.

BRIEF CASE: Emma

Emma bought a ticket for a day trip to London, saying that she wanted to travel on the next train, leaving in 15 minutes. When the inspector checked her ticket on the train, she asked Emma to pay a further £6, as she had been undercharged by the booking clerk. Although Emma claimed that it was the train operating company's mistake in selling her the wrong ticket, by law she had to pay the difference. When a contract is made, one side cannot gain by the other side's genuine mistake.

cars and motorcycles

Getting started

The licence

It is an offence to drive or ride a motor vehicle without the correct licence. You get a full driving licence when you have passed your test, and the licence will be valid until you are 70. Licences for drivers over 70 are issued for three years at a time.

New licences are now the size of a credit card and contain the holder's photograph. Old paper licences will be changed to the new format when they are renewed or if the details need to be changed. You must tell DVLA (see **contacts**) of any change of address immediately – or risk a fine.

If you want to learn to drive, you need a provisional driving licence. Application forms are available from post offices. When you get your licence, sign it immediately – don't drive until you have done so. Car drivers can hold the same provisional licence until they are 70. A motorcyclist's provisional licence is only valid for two years.

Learning to drive a car

When you are driving on a provisional licence you must display 'L' plates ('D' plates in Wales), which should be removed or covered up when the vehicle is not being driven by a learner. You must not drive on a motorway, and you must have someone with you in the front passenger seat of the car who is over 21 and has held a full EU driving licence in the relevant category for three years. This person must be fit to drive and must not have had more than the legal amount of alcohol.

The driving test is in three parts: a written theory exam, an online hazard perception test and a practical test. The theory paper, which must be passed before taking the practical test, lasts 40 minutes and is made up of 35 multiple-choice

questions. More information is available from the 'Motoring' section of the Directgov website, www.direct.gov.uk.

Learning to ride a motorcycle, moped or scooter

The starting point for all riders of moped and motorcycles is a Compulsory Basic Training course, which must be completed before a moped or motorcycle is taken on the road. (The only exception is for drivers who passed their car test before 1 February 2001, who can ride a moped without L-plates and without taking the CBT course.)

Once you have completed the CBT you can go on to take the theory and practical tests to qualify for a full moped or motorcycle licence.

You can ride a moped on the road from the age of 16, but cannot take up a full moped licence until you are 17. This is also the minimum age for learning to ride a motorcycle, which must be on a machine with an engine size no larger than 125ccs, and a maximum power output of 11kw. There are two types of motorcycle licence. One restricts the rider to less powerful machines; the other allows the rider after two years to ride any size of motorcycle. See **contacts** for more detailed information.

Learner motorcyclists may not ride on a motorway, nor carry a pillion passenger, unless the passenger is also licensed to ride that type of machine. Mopeds, scooters, and motorised skateboards cannot be used on the public roads without a licence, road tax and insurance.

MOT

Most vehicles that are three or more years old must pass an MOT test if they are to be used or left on the road.

Road tax

A car or motorbike must display a current tax disc, whether it is being used or just standing on the road. The fine for breaking this regulation is normally about twice the cost of the disc. The Driving and Vehicle Licensing Agency (known as the DVLA), now have powers to wheel clamp and remove vehicles not showing a current disc, and to charge a fee for their release. It is a crime to use a tax disc belonging to another vehicle.

If your vehicle is being kept off the road and not taxed, you will need to make a Statutory Off Road Notification (SORN). You can do this online at the Directgov website, or tel 0870 850 4444.

Insurance

It is an offence to drive, ride or even place a motor vehicle on the road without insurance. The penalties for this are very heavy, and it makes no difference for someone to say it was a genuine mistake and that they thought they were insured. Failure to have insurance means a fine and penalty points on a licence, and possible disqualification.

It is also an offence for someone to allow their car or motorcycle to be used by a person who is not insured to drive it.

There are three different kinds of motor insurance, offering different levels of cover:

- **third party insurance only pays for damage caused to other people or their property (and not to your own vehicle). This is the minimum level of insurance cover required by law;**
- **third party fire and theft gives you further protection by covering your vehicle against theft or fire damage;**
- **fully comprehensive insurance is usually the most expensive, but covers the cost of accident repair damage to your vehicle as well as compensating you and others for injuries or damage in the accident.**

When you apply for any insurance, make sure the information you give is accurate and complete. If it's not, your insurance will be invalid. It's an offence knowingly to make a false statement to obtain insurance. For more information, see **money**, pages 66–67.

BRIEF CASE: Sarah

Sarah bought a Morgan sports car, and insured it for her and her fiancé to drive. The car, worth £26,000, was stolen. When she claimed on her insurance, it came to light that her fiancé had received a serious motoring conviction several years ago, which Sarah had failed to mention on the application form. The insurance policy was therefore not valid, and Sarah received no compensation for the loss of her car.

cars and motorcycles

AT WHAT AGE?

At 14 you can ride an electrically powered pedal cycle.

At 16 you can ride a moped up to 50cc, a small tractor, mowing machine or invalid car. If you receive a disability living allowance, you can also drive a car.

At 17 you can drive a car with up to 8 passenger seats, a motor tricycle, a motorcycle up to 125cc, a large tractor and a van or lorry up to 3.5 tons.

At 18 you can drive a van or lorry up to 7.5 tons.

At 21 you can drive all other vehicles. For hiring a car, most car hire companies have a minimum age of 21 or 23.

Traffic offences

Every vehicle on the road must meet a whole set of regulations covering brakes, tyres, lights, mirrors, steering and even windscreen washer bottles (which must, by law, never be empty). A police officer may stop a vehicle at any time to check that it is in roadworthy condition, and it is no excuse for the driver to claim that they didn't realise a light wasn't working. These are absolute offences and apply even if the driver was completely unaware of the problem.

If the police believe a vehicle is not roadworthy, they can instruct the driver to get it checked and repaired by a garage (usually within 14 days), give the driver a fixed penalty or call up a specially trained vehicle examiner to inspect the car or bike there and then. A police officer who feels a vehicle is so dangerous that someone will probably be injured if it is used any further, can immediately ban it from being driven.

Cycling

Cyclists are expected to follow the same basic laws as other road users. They have a duty of care to pedestrians, other riders and road users. It is an offence, under the *Highways Act 1835*, to ride a bicycle (or tricycle) on the pavement – a law that applies to riders of all ages. Police officers now have the power to impose a £30 fixed penalty notice on cyclists over 16 who ride on the pavement. It is also against the law to wheel a bike past a red traffic light or to ride it across a zebra crossing.

It is an offence to ride under the influence of alcohol or drugs. There is no breath test for cyclists; a court would instead be guided by evidence from the officer who made the arrest.

BUYING A CAR

- A small popular car is usually less of a risk. Spare parts are cheaper and easier to obtain, insurance costs lower and it will probably be easier to sell when you want to change it.
- A car bought privately is usually cheaper than one bought from a dealer, but you have fewer rights if things go wrong. The *Sale of Goods Act 1979* gives greater protection if you buy from a dealer. A car bought privately need not be 'of satisfactory quality' but only be 'as described' (see money page 54). The legal expression 'caveat emptor' (meaning 'buyer beware'), particularly applies when buying a second-hand car. It is notoriously difficult to get problems sorted out once you have paid for the car.
- Look at the car in daylight. Take someone along with you who knows about cars. Check the owner's purchase documents to see if any hire-purchase payments are still due. For between £100–£300 the RAC, AA or Green Flag will inspect and report on the mechanical state of the car, check on the HP payments, whether the car has been stolen or is an insurance write-off. HPI Autodata or AA Car Data provide a similar service at a slightly lower cost, without the mechanical inspection.
- Look to see if the car's mileage tallies with the MOT certificate and the service history. You can also check with previous owners. Ask the dealer if they have tried to verify the mileage – they have to do this by law. Be wary if there is a sticker on the speedometer indicating that there is no guarantee that the mileage is accurate.
- Ask to see the Vehicle Registration Document or Certificate (V5C). If it's a private sale, it should contain the seller's name and address. It also gives the Vehicle Identification Number (VIN), which should correspond with the number stamped on identification plates under the bonnet and on the floor. If you have any doubts, leave the car alone.
- If you buy a car that turns out to be stolen, it generally remains the property of the true owner – meaning that you will almost certainly lose your money, unless you can get it back from the person from whom you bought the car.

BRIEF CASE: Anna

Anna went to look at a Ford Escort, advertised privately in her local paper. She asked the seller if the car had been in an accident. He said no, but having bought the car, Anna later found evidence of major crash repairs. She went back to the seller, pointed out the car was not as described and eventually got her money back.

However, if the car had just been unreliable (even breaking down on her first drive), there is probably little she could have done, as there is nothing in law that states that a car bought privately must be of satisfactory or reasonable quality.

driving

Safety

Seat belts and crash helmets

Seat belts (front and rear), where fitted, must be worn by drivers and passengers in all vehicles, including minibuses and coaches. If a passenger in your car does not wear a belt, it is he or she who will be prosecuted, not you – unless the passenger is under 14, when it is your responsibility. Children who are under 12 and below 4'5" tall must sit on a safety seat or booster cushion.

Motorcyclist and pillion passengers must both wear an approved safety helmet on all journeys. This regulation does not apply to a follower of the Sikh religion while he is wearing a turban. Tinted visors may only be used during daylight hours.

SPEED LIMITS

Cars and motorcycles are limited to

- **30 mph in built-up areas,**
- **60 mph on single carriageways,**
- **70 mph on dual carriageways and motorways.**

The presence of street lights generally means that a 30mph speed limit is in operation unless otherwise indicated.

Speeding

Speeding is an absolute offence, which means that it is no defence to say that it wasn't dangerous or that you didn't realise that you were breaking the speed limit. Nor is there much point in denying that you were travelling at the speed the police say you were, unless you can prove it. You will usually be given a fixed penalty and penalty points.

If you break the speed limit, or are seen by the police to be driving carelessly or dangerously, you must be warned of the possibility of prosecution at the time of the offence or served with a summons within 14 days of the offence. Otherwise you cannot be convicted, unless an accident occurred at the time or immediately after.

Driving badly

Careless driving is to drive in a way that is not how a careful and reasonable driver would behave. Pulling out from a side road without looking is an example of this.

Dangerous driving is to drive in a way that is dangerous to people or property, such as driving very fast through a built-up area or overtaking on a sharp bend. Dangerous driving and causing death by dangerous driving are very serious offences, which courts will punish with fines, disqualification, and imprisonment. If you face such a charge, get in touch with a solicitor straightaway.

Stolen vehicles

Stealing a vehicle to sell on to someone else is theft. Joyriding, or taking a car to ride around in and then dumping it, is a different offence known as 'taking a vehicle without the owner's consent' or TWOC. Both are punishable by a fine or imprisonment.

Joyriding

The *Aggravated Vehicle-Taking Act 1992* gives courts powers to deal with joyriders who drive dangerously and are involved in an accident causing injury and damage. A sentence of up to five years' imprisonment may be imposed, with a year's automatic disqualification from driving.

Mobile phones

It is an offence to use a hand-held mobile phone while driving – which includes waiting at traffic lights or in a traffic jam – except to call 999 or 112 in a genuine emergency. Motorists may be fined £60 (fixed penalty) and have three penalty points added to their licence, with punishments rising to £1,000 if convicted in court, and £2,500 for drivers of vans and lorries.

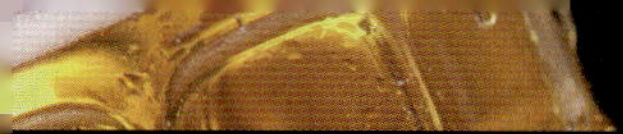

BRIEF CASE: Peter

Peter was involved in a crash with a motorcycle. He feared that it was his fault and that he would lose his licence, as he already had a number of penalty points. He persuaded his wife Sophie, who was not in the car at the time, to tell the police that it was she who was driving. A week later they both admitted the deception, but were charged with perverting the course of justice. Peter and Sophie were sentenced to four and two months in prison.

Drinking and driving Alcohol seriously affects a driver's judgement and reactions. There is no law that limits a driver to a certain number of drinks, such as two pints of beer or one glass of wine, but there is a maximum amount of alcohol that you may have in your body while driving or being in charge of a car. In law, being in charge of a car includes simply sitting in the driving seat of a parked car.

The limits The amount of alcohol in a person's body is measured in their breath, blood, or urine.

Breath tests The police will carry out a roadside breath test to check whether a driver has more than the permitted amount of alcohol in their body. Uniformed police can breathalyse anyone whom they reasonably suspect of driving with excess alcohol, who is involved in a traffic offence or road accident, however minor, even if there is no suspicion of alcohol. A uniformed police officer is also quite entitled to stop motorists at random in order to see whether there is a reasonable suspicion that they have consumed any alcohol. If there is, the officer can go on to ask the motorist to take a breath test.

If the test is positive or the driver refuses a breath test, the driver will be arrested and taken to a police station for further tests.

No escape A driver who fails to blow into the device properly, or refuses to take a test, will still end up with a heavy fine and have his or her licence endorsed with three to eleven penalty points. Courts rarely accept that there are special reasons for drivers being over the limit. Disqualification from driving is almost automatic. A drunken driver who causes someone's death may be sent to prison for up to ten years, and will be disqualified from driving for at least two years.

BRIEF CASE: Paul

Paul had had a few drinks when he was phoned by a friend who had run out of petrol, miles from anywhere, with his old and sick mother. Paul got into his car to go and fetch them, but was stopped by the police and breathalysed positive. Although he told the court that it was an emergency, the magistrates still found Paul guilty of drinking and driving, saying that the police, RAC or AA could instead have been called to help.

driving

Penalty points The police and courts deal with most motoring offences through a system of penalty points that are entered on a driver's licence. Anyone receiving twelve or more points within a period of three years will almost always be disqualified from driving for at least six months. Details of the points carried for each offence are given in the Highway Code. Drivers who have six or more penalty points on their licence within two years of their test go back to being a learner until they pass a further test. People disqualified for two years or more can, after a minimum period, apply to the court to have their disqualification reduced.

accidents

What to do Accidents happen to the most careful of drivers, often through no fault of their own. If you are involved in an accident, there are certain things that you should and should not do…

- Stop immediately. Try to stay calm, even if people are yelling and screaming at you.
- Check that everyone involved in the accident is OK. If anyone is injured, call an ambulance before you do anything else.
- You must give your name and address and details of your vehicle to anyone who has reasonable need to know them. This includes a police officer at the scene of the accident, anyone who is injured, anyone whose property is damaged and the owner of any animal injured or killed. (This applies to horses, cows, sheep, goats and dogs – but not cats.) If someone is injured, you must also produce your insurance certificate to show that you are properly insured. If you can't do this at the time of the accident, then you must give this information to the police as soon as possible, and certainly within 24 hours. If you don't, you will be committing an offence.
- Make sure you get the name, address, vehicle registration number and insurance details of the other drivers involved.
- Contact your insurance company as soon as possible, and also make a detailed note of everything that happened. This should cover the time of day, weather, light, estimated speeds, position of vehicles before and after the accident, what people said and anything else that you think might be relevant. If you can, take photos before anything is moved, or draw a sketch plan as soon as you feel able to do so.
- Don't drive away without stopping. It is a criminal offence.
- Be cautious if the other driver suggests not calling the police and offers you cash to cover the damage. It might be an offence not to report the accident, and you may find that the damage to your vehicle costs a lot more than you are being offered. If someone is injured in the accident it is an offence not to report it to the police.
- Don't admit it was your fault. You may find later that the other driver was drunk, driving too fast, or without lights – in which case you might not be to blame at all. If you do admit responsibility, your words may end up being used against you in court and may affect your insurance claim.

 CONTACTS see pages 152–159 for organisations able to give help & advice

young citizen's passport

police and courts

INDIVIDUALS ENGAGING IN SOCIETY

Citizenship Foundation

powers and duties

Most of the information that the police receives comes from the general public. Without this help they could do very little.

Much of the law setting out police powers and duties is contained in the *Police and Criminal Evidence Act 1984*, known as PACE. Under this law, the government publishes guidelines, called Codes of Practice, which the police must follow when searching for and collecting evidence. If the police do not follow these rules when questioning a suspect, the judge or magistrate may decide that the evidence obtained cannot be used in court, and the police officers concerned may be disciplined.

Copies of the Codes of Practice are available from the Home Office, (see **contacts**), libraries, and every police station. Anyone detained by the police has a right to read them.

POLICE DISCIPLINE

Police officers must obey both the law of the land, and their own code of discipline. This discipline code is broken if an officer…

- **unreasonably neglects their duty;**
- **makes a false written or spoken statement;**
- **misuses their authority, e.g. through unnecessary violence;**
- **is rude, abusive or racially discriminates against someone.**

The police have a legal duty to promote racial equality and good relations between people of different racial groups.

stop and search

Stop! If a police officer stops you in the street, you are entitled to know the officer's name and the police station where they work. Normally you are also entitled to know why you have been stopped. It is not acceptable for this to be because of your colour, dress, hairstyle, or that you have been in trouble before.

Strictly speaking, you don't have to answer a police officer's questions. But if you refuse to give your name and address, you may be arrested if the officer believes you have something to hide.

A person who is driving a motor vehicle, or is suspected of committing a crime or some kind of anti-social behaviour, *must* give their name and address, but need not say any more. They have the right not to answer any more questions until they have received legal advice, see page 117.

Stay calm If you're stopped by the police, keep calm and don't overreact. If you're obstructive or rude, you're more likely to be arrested. Staying calm will also help you remember what happened and what was said. If you deliberately mislead the police by giving false information or wasting their time, you risk a fine or even imprisonment.

Search!

People The police do not have the power to search anyone they choose, but they can search someone (and the vehicle in which they are travelling) who has been arrested or is suspected of carrying:

- **illegal drugs;**
- **stolen goods, or goods on which duty has not been paid;**
- **weapons, or anything that might be used as a weapon;**
- **anything that might be used for theft, burglary, deception, joyriding, causing criminal damage, or hunting or poaching animals.**

Any search involving more than a check of your outer clothing should be done out of public view or in a police station or van. If the search requires more than the removal of outer clothing, it should be done by someone of the same sex. The way the search is carried out can depend on what the police are looking for. For example, the police may decide to make an intimate search of someone suspected of carrying drugs – given the possibility that the drugs are being hidden inside the person's body.

In the know If you, or the vehicle in which you are travelling, are searched by the police, the officers should state beforehand why the search is taking place and what they expect to find. You have every right to ask for an explanation if this has not been made clear. If the police search you illegally, they are committing an assault. But if they have good reason, and you refuse, you may be charged with obstruction.

The police should normally make a written record of the search. You can ask for a copy of this at any time within the next year.

Special powers Police powers of search in certain circumstances were extended by the *Criminal Justice and Public Order Act 1994*. If a senior police officer believes that a serious violent incident might take place or that dangerous weapons are being carried, he or she can give officers the authority to stop any person or vehicle in the area to search for the weapons. This applies even when the constable has no grounds for suspecting that the person stopped might have broken the law. With the authority of an officer of the rank of inspector or above, officers may remove and seize anything covering a person's face if they reasonably believe it is being used to hide the person's identity.

If you are stopped in this way, you are again entitled to request a written record of the search within a year. Failing to stop when asked by a police officer can result in a fine or imprisonment.

stop and search

Property

The police do not have the power to enter and search any house or building that they choose. But they are allowed to carry out a search if:

- **they have the agreement of the occupier of the building; or**
- **they have reason to believe they might find someone who has committed an offence, or to look for relevant evidence in a property that was used by someone before they were arrested; or**
- **they have a warrant (or permission) from a court; or**
- **in order to catch an escaped prisoner, save life, prevent serious property damage or to prevent certain kinds of disturbance.**

If possible, the police should explain why they are making the search and keep a record of how they got into the property, damage caused, and anything they took away. Other officials, such as environmental health officers, may also enter and search the property if they are named on the warrant and accompanied by a police officer. If the search is unlawful, it may be possible to get compensation, but this is not easy.

arrest

When the police make an arrest, they are taking the person under the care and control of the law. This means that, for the time being, the suspect loses certain freedoms – such as to go and do as they please – but, in return, has certain rights designed to protect them from unreasonable treatment. If you are arrested and taken to a police station, you are entitled to:

- **know the reason for your arrest;**
- **see a solicitor;**
- **have someone told where you are;**
- **read a copy of the Codes of Practice, which explain the procedures the police should follow when questioning you.**

You should be given a written note of these rights and cautioned, see page 119. You cannot normally be held for more than 24 hours without being charged or released. But if it is a serious offence, this may be extended by up to twelve hours by a senior police officer or 96 hours with the approval of a magistrates' court.

HELPING THE POLICE WITH THEIR ENQUIRIES

If you are asked to go to a police station to help with enquiries, it's important to know if you are being arrested, or whether the decision to attend is up to you. If you are being asked to go voluntarily, you may refuse – although the police may then decide to arrest you, and then you have to go.

You are entitled to send a message to your family or a friend telling them where you are, and to receive free legal advice from a solicitor, even though you are attending the police station voluntarily.

If you have not been arrested and go to the police station voluntarily, you may leave at any time you wish.

at the police station

Legal advice

In almost all circumstances, anyone who has been arrested, or who goes to a police station voluntarily, is entitled to private legal advice from the solicitor on duty or a solicitor of their own choice. The consultation with the duty solicitor is free. Information on your rights should be given to you by the police.

If you have been arrested, or are being questioned about an offence, or if you feel at all unsure about your legal position, it is better not to answer questions (except your name and address) until you have had a chance to speak to a solicitor.

With the approval of a senior officer, the police can delay access to a solicitor chosen by the detained person (but not to the duty solicitor) for up to 36 hours (48 hours in cases of suspected terrorism), if this might interfere with the evidence, endanger or alert others, or hinder the recovery of property obtained as a result of the offence.

SOLICITORS

Solicitors give advice on legal problems. They can take action for you on your behalf and represent you in court – although in a higher court this may be done by a barrister.

Solicitors can advise and represent their clients in matters of criminal *and* civil law. There are solicitors' offices in every town and city in England and Wales.

Costs Legal advice from the duty solicitor at a police station is free. If you are charged with a criminal offence, but not held in custody, you should try to see a solicitor as soon as possible, who will advise and help you apply for free representation if your case goes to court.

If you need the help of a solicitor on a civil matter, it is important to find a solicitor who specialises in cases involving your particular problem. The Law Society, the Community Legal Advice service and your local Citizens Advice Bureau can give you the name of firms in your area that will be able to help.

As a general rule, solicitors charge for their services. However, financial help may be available from public funds for certain kinds of cases. When you first make contact with a solicitor it is important to ask about the financial arrangements and what you will be expected to pay. Some solicitors will give a free introductory interview in which all of this can be explained.

Questioning

If you are under 17, the police should not normally interview you without your parent or an 'appropriate adult' present. An appropriate adult is someone who knows you, such as a relative, adult friend or social worker.

If you have been arrested, you must give the police your name and address, but, after that, you have the right to stay silent and not answer any further questions. However, if the case goes to trial, the court will be told of this and it may strengthen the case against you. If you refuse to answer questions in court, the magistrates or jury are allowed to take this into account in deciding whether or not you are guilty.

There are clear rules governing the way police officers can question a person, designed to stop unfair pressure being placed on a suspect.

There should be regular breaks for food and the cell and interview room should be clean, properly heated, ventilated, and lit. Bedding should be clean, and washing and toilet facilities must be provided. Someone who is deaf, has speech difficulties, or has difficulty in understanding English should be given a signer or an interpreter.

If, after questioning, the police decide to arrest you, they should give you written information about your legal rights.

The caution

Once a police officer has reason to believe that you have committed an offence, they must caution you by saying: '*You do not have to say anything. But it may harm your defence if you do not mention when questioned something which you later rely on in court. Anything you do say may be given in evidence.*'

Tape recording

Your interview at the police station will probably be recorded on tape. The officer will begin with questions about your name and address, and should explain the reason for your interview and give details about the offence on which you are being questioned.

If the interview is not recorded, notes should be made by the officer concerned. You have the right to see these and sign them if you agree that they are a fair record of what was said. You can also ask for a copy of the custody record.

Fingerprints and photographs

Fingerprints and other non-intimate samples such as saliva, footwear impressions, and photos can be taken without your consent. If a person does not cooperate, reasonable force can be used. Intimate samples such as blood, urine and dental impressions require your written consent and the consent of the inspector. However, refusal to give consent may harm your defence if you are to go to trial.

charge, caution, release

Charged

After questioning you, the police must decide what to do next. If there appears to be enough evidence, they can:

- **charge you with the offence; or**
- **send the papers to the Crown Prosecution Service, for them to decide whether to charge you; or**
- **issue you with a reprimand or warning if you are under 18; or**
- **issue you with an informal warning, or a formal or conditional caution if you are 18 or over.**

If you are charged, you will be given a charge sheet indicating the nature of the offence, when and where you are due to appear in court and the conditions of your bail.

Once you are charged you should not be asked any further questions except in certain specified situations, for example, when new information has come to light.

Bail

If you are charged with an offence, the law states that you should normally be released on bail, unless the police believe you should be held:

- **because they believe you have not given your correct name and address;**
- **for the protection of others, to stop you committing another offence, or to stop you interfering in their investigations;**
- **for your own protection (or, if you are under 18, because it is in your own interests); or**
- **to make sure you turn up in court.**

If you are not released by the police, you must be brought before a magistrate at the earliest opportunity, who will decide whether you can be released on bail and, if so, whether conditions should apply. For example, you may be required to report to the police station once a week, or to have someone provide a financial guarantee that you will be present in court when required. If you are refused bail, or conditions are applied, the court must give reasons for this decision. A person who breaks their bail will be returned to custody and is unlikely to get or be given bail again.

Anyone who is charged with, or already convicted of, murder, attempted murder, manslaughter, rape or attempted rape, will only be given bail in exceptional circumstances. Courts also need not grant bail if the defendant was already on bail when the offence was committed.

Reprimand, warning or caution

These are strongly worded warnings given to an offender by a senior police officer, designed to remind them that they will almost certainly be sent to court if they commit further offences. A reprimand, warning or caution may be made only if the accused admits their guilt.

Reprimands or warnings are given to young people below the age of 18. Someone who has received a reprimand or warning and who offends again will normally be charged.

Offenders aged 18 or over, may receive either an informal warning, or a formal or conditional caution. Offenders who receive a caution are warned that they will almost certainly be sent to court if they commit a further offence. A conditional caution will have conditions attached – such as compensating the victim, cleaning graffiti or taking treatment for drug dependency – in an attempt to stop the person from re-offending. Both formal and conditional cautions form part of an offender's criminal record.

COMPLAINTS AGAINST THE POLICE

If you feel that you have suffered, or witnessed police misconduct, you may decide that you want to make an official complaint. This should be done within one year of the incident.

Think about what happened; make sure you are clear what was wrong. If it is a serious matter, it is a good idea to speak to a solicitor or your local Citizens Advice Bureau beforehand. The Independent Police Complaints Commission (an independent organisation that oversees public complaints against police officers) can give advice on the type of things that you should put into a complaint, and information on how the complaint will be investigated, see contacts.

You can make your complaint in person at any police station, or by writing to the Chief Constable of the police force concerned or to the IPCC.

In reply, you may get an apology or an explanation of the officer's conduct. If you are not satisfied with this, or your complaint is of a serious nature, there may be a full investigation supervised by the IPCC.

ANTI-SOCIAL BEHAVIOUR ORDERS

An ASBO, or anti-social behaviour order, is an order issued by a court commonly prohibiting someone from entering a certain area or spending time with a particular group of people. ASBOs are designed to stop behaviour that causes people distress or alarm, and can be used with anyone aged 10 or above.

The local council or police will normally apply to a court for an ASBO – and the orders are used to try to control all kinds of anti-social behaviour. An ASBO is effective for a minimum of two years and it is a criminal offence to break it.

Acceptable behaviour contracts

An acceptable behaviour contract is an agreement made between a young person, their parent or carer, and a local agency, such as the police, social services or a housing authority. The contract will list the kinds of anti-social behaviour that the person promises not to do again, along with any other measures that they (and their parent or carer) agree to undertake.

Fixed Penalty Notices

Under the *Criminal Justice and Police Act 2001*, police officers have the power to issue a fine, known as a fixed penalty notice, to anyone committing certain minor offences, including drunken behaviour, dropping litter and throwing fireworks. The fine must be paid within 21 days and a notice can be given to anyone aged 10 and above. Fines can range from £50–£80, and once the fine is paid, the person is no longer liable for conviction and does not have a criminal record.

BRIEF CASE: No returns

A family of five were each issued with an anti-social behaviour order banning them from entering the Borough of Wirral in Cheshire where they used to live, after they subjected the local residents to a barrage of verbal abuse, threats and violent behaviour.

terrorism

Most terrorist offences are already against the law, but the police now have extra powers to help them with their enquiries.

Definition

Terrorism refers to actions designed to advance a political, religious or ideological cause, which deliberately:

- **cause serious violence or damage;**
- **threaten or intimidate members of the public;**
- **create a public health or safety risk;**
- **interfere with electronic communications.**

Police powers

The police can use stop and search powers to see if someone is a terrorist, even if they do not have any grounds for suspecting the person of committing an offence.

They can specify areas where, for up to 28 days, people and vehicles may be randomly stopped and searched by an officer in uniform without evidence of illegal activity.

When investigating a terrorist offence, premises can be searched without a warrant and a senior police officer can authorise emergency searches if it is believed to be 'in the interests of the state'.

Areas can be cordoned off to allow the police to search for evidence of terrorism.

Detention

Terrorist suspects can be detained by the police without charge for up to 28 days.

Access to a solicitor can be delayed for 48 hours. This also applies to a suspect's right to contact a friend or relative to tell them that they have been arrested.

Under the *Prevention of Terrorism Act 2005*, the government can place people they suspect of terrorism under house arrest, even without the evidence to go to court to prove an offence.

Other powers

Some organisations are forbidden – known as 'proscribed' – which means that it is illegal to be a member of them. The list contains suspected terrorist organisations from around the world.

Since the bomb attacks in London in July 2005, the police have been given extra powers under the *Terrorism Act 2006*. It is now an offence to prepare a terrorist act, to give or receive terrorist training, and to sell or distribute terrorist publications.

'Praising or celebrating' terrorism in a way which could encourage others to carry out a terrorist act can lead to being arrested and charged with 'glorification' of terrorism.

Crown Prosecution Service

The job of investigating a crime and charging a suspect is done by the police, but the decision as to whether to continue with the case and bring it to court is made by the Crown Prosecution Service (CPS). This is an independent prosecuting service, made up of trained lawyers, who decide whether there is a realistic chance of conviction and whether the seriousness of the crime merits a trial. If the answer to either of these questions is 'no', the case will be dropped.

It is difficult to predict the amount of time it will take to investigate and bring a case to court. If you are charged with an offence normally heard in a magistrates' court, you should know within six months whether you are to be prosecuted.

In certain areas of the country, experimental limits have been set on the amount of time someone under 18 has to wait between their arrest and first appearance in court (36 days), and between their conviction and sentence (29 days). These limits have not yet been introduced nationally.

Charge or summons

You will be told of the date and time of your first appearance in court on the police charge sheet or by summons through the post.

If you are 17 or under, your case will normally be heard in a youth court. If you are 18 or over, your first appearance will be in the local adult magistrates' court.

Youth court

If the accused is under 18, the case must normally be heard in a youth court.

If a young person is charged jointly with an adult the trial may be held in a magistrates' court or, in serious cases such as murder, in the Crown Court.

A youth court is made up of either a District Judge sitting alone, or three magistrates (which must include one man and one woman), trained to deal with cases involving young people.

If the accused is under 16, their parents must attend the court. Parents of 16 or 17-year-olds may also be ordered to attend.

Members of the public are not allowed in a youth court to listen to the case, nor can the identity or pictures of any young person concerned in the trial be published in the press.

Magistrates' court

All criminal cases pass through magistrates' courts, in some way or another. Normally three magistrates sit in court. Also known as justices of the peace, they are usually not lawyers, but members of the local community. Magistrates will reach a verdict and pass sentence themselves on all cases involving less serious offences (known as summary offences). More serious cases are dealt with by the Crown Court (with a jury), but before they reach this stage, it is the magistrates' job to decide whether there is enough evidence for the accused to stand trial. There are some offences that can be heard by either a magistrates' or Crown Court, and the accused can decide which to choose.

Crown Court

This is the court where more serious offences are heard. A judge takes charge of the hearing to make sure that the evidence is properly presented, but the verdict is reached by the jury. The judge will pass sentence if the defendant is found guilty and is generally able to impose longer sentences than a magistrates' court. The sentence is decided by taking into account any maximum set by law, the circumstances surrounding the case, previous convictions, and possibly the background of the defendant, if it is thought to have any bearing on the case.

There are procedures set out to ensure that a young person accused of a crime is not made to feel intimidated by the experience and receives a fair trial.

Age of criminal responsibility

A child under the age of ten who breaks the law cannot be charged with the crime. However, children under ten who are out of control can be made subject to a child safety order (placing them under the supervision of a social worker or a member of a youth offending team) or a care order (taking them into care).

courts

Criminal Defence Service

Help with the cost of legal advice and the presentation of your case in court is provided by the Criminal Defence Service.

If you are charged with an offence, it is important to get legal advice as soon as possible. You may wish to use the solicitor that you saw at the police station, or you can consult another one. Solicitors must hold a contract from the Legal Services Commission (LSC) in order to carry out this work. You can find a contracted firm by phoning the LSC or searching the Community Legal Service website, see **contacts**.

There are different types of help available, which your solicitor will be able to explain. If you are to be tried in a magistrates' or the Crown Court you may be able to get help with the cost of a solicitor, and possibly a barrister, to prepare and present your case. Depending on your income and savings, you may be required to make a contribution towards the cost.

If you find yourself in court without anyone to give you advice, you can ask to see the duty solicitor who can give you free advice and representation on your first appearance. You could also ask the magistrates to delay your case until you've had time to talk to someone, though they will probably want to know why you did not sort it out earlier. It is always best if possible to get advice before you go to court.

The Court Service

If you need to go to court, for example as a witness or juror, and need information on what you can expect or what you might have to do, your local court should be able to help (see Courts in the phone book). Further details are given in the Courts' Charter, see **contacts**.

Juries

The job of a jury, which sits in a Crown Court, is to decide on the facts of a criminal case and on the guilt or innocence of the accused. It is made up of 12 adults, aged between 18–70, who have lived in Britain for a continuous period of five years from the age of 13. They are chosen at random from the local Electoral Register (see **law, government and human rights**, page 134), but there are certain categories of people who cannot be selected. These include anyone on bail, anyone who has been convicted of a serious criminal offence and anyone who has had a prison sentence or detention order in the last ten years.

If you are called as a member of a jury, you will usually be given about six weeks' notice. Normally it is compulsory. But if there is a strong reason why you are unable to serve – such as exams, a holiday which has been already booked, the care of a relative or major problems at work – then you may be excused or allowed to defer your service until later in the year, although it is important to request this as soon as possible.

Jurors are able to claim the cost of travel to Court and a small financial allowance. There is information for jurors on the Court Service websites, see **contacts**.

young citizen's passport

law
government and human rights

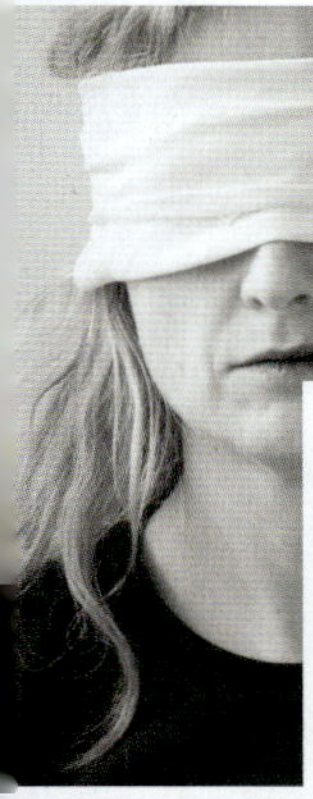

INDIVIDUALS ENGAGING IN SOCIETY

Citizenship Foundation

making the law

Parliament

Between 30 and 50 major new laws are passed by Parliament each year. Starting as a Bill, each one must be debated and voted on by the House of Commons and the House of Lords before becoming law. The House of Lords can recommend changes and delay the progress of a Bill, but it can't actually stop it from being passed. The only Bill that the House of Lords can reject is one that tries to extend a Parliament's life beyond five years (the maximum time between general elections) – a protection against power being seized by a dictator.

After going through both Houses of Parliament, a Bill becomes an Act (or statute) by being given the royal assent by the Queen. Today this is merely a formality. The last monarch to refuse to approve an Act was Queen Anne in 1707.

Most Bills are put to Parliament by the Government as part of its manifesto, or overall policy. A small number are presented by individual MPs and peers, known as private members' Bills. Few of these become law, as there is only a limited amount of time to debate and vote on them. Most of Parliament's time is spent on Government business. Committees of MPs, known as Select Committees, monitor and question what Ministers and their departments do.

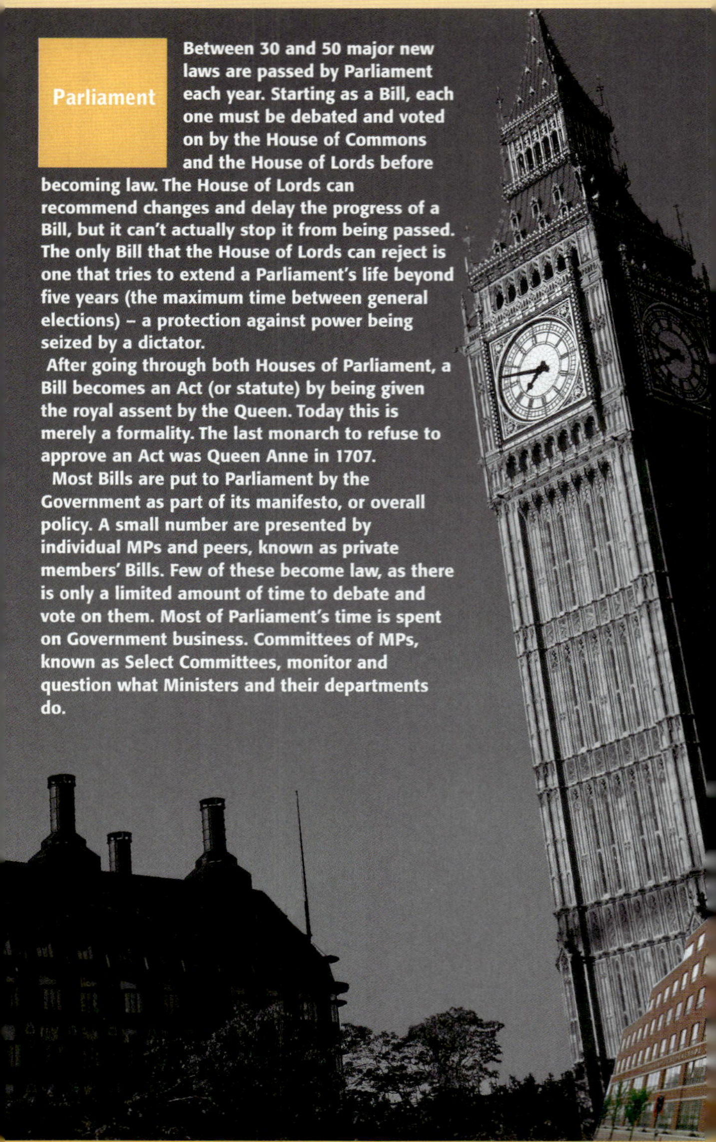

European law

As part of its membership of the European Union, the UK applies all new laws agreed by EU member states. This is explained in **the european parliament**, pages 148–149.

Courts

When a case comes to court, the magistrates or judge normally apply the law in the same way as courts have done in the past. This is called a system of precedent and ensures that similar cases are dealt with in a consistent way. However, there are times when the circumstances of a case have not arisen before, or when the senior judges decide that existing judgments do not reflect modern society. In these situations, by their decision, judges can create or change the law.

The National Assembly for Wales

Elections for the 60 members who make up the Welsh Assembly (AMs) take place every four years. All laws for Wales are still passed by Parliament in London, although the Assembly can debate and give its views on issues directly affecting Wales. It also has responsibility for deciding how laws affecting, for example, education, health, industry, agriculture, transport, training and environment, are put into practice in Wales. Questions of foreign affairs, defence, taxation, social security and broadcasting are decided for the whole of the United Kingdom by the Government in London.

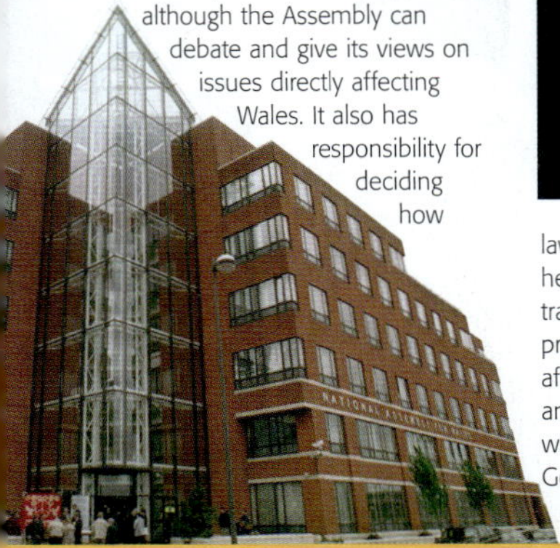

BRIEF CASE

A month after separating from his wife, a man broke into her parents' house where she was staying and tried to have sex with her against her will. The husband was found guilty of attempted rape and sentenced to five years in prison. He appealed on the grounds that a husband could not be found guilty of raping his wife. The case went up to the House of Lords where it was heard by five senior judges. They decided that the rule that a husband could not rape his wife (which went back to before 1736) should no longer be part of the law, since a husband and wife were now seen as equal partners in marriage. As a result the law was changed and a man who forces his wife to have sexual intercourse against her will may now be guilty of rape.

European Convention on Human Rights

This is an international agreement drawn up by the Council of Europe to protect people's human rights after the horrors of the Second World War. It took effect in 1953 and sets out fundamental rights and freedoms that everybody should have and the limited circumstances when the state may interfere with those freedoms. These include a right to liberty, a right to a fair trial, privacy, freedom of speech etc. The Council of Europe represents a wider group of countries than the EU.

Anyone who believes the law in this country has not dealt fairly with their rights can take their case to the European Court of Human Rights in Strasbourg. The UK has agreed to abide by the findings of the Strasbourg Court but this is a long and costly process. Before the *Human Rights Act 1998* came into force, the UK courts themselves had no power to deal with human rights cases.

BRIEF CASE

In September 1976 Jeffrey, aged 16, took a short cut home from his school in Scotland through a nearby cemetery. This was against school rules and Jeffrey was reported to the head, who decided that he should be punished with the strap. The boy refused. He was supported by his parents, who said that they thought corporal punishment was morally wrong. Jeffrey was suspended.

Both the school and the local authority suggested various ways in which he might be allowed back – but could not promise that Jeffrey would never be beaten for misbehaviour. Jeffrey's parents would not agree to this. They claimed that the local authority were breaking part of the European Convention on Human Rights, which says that no one shall be denied the right to education and that parents have the right to make sure that their children are taught in a way that respects their religious and philosophical beliefs.

When the case eventually reached the European Court of Human Rights in 1982, the Court agreed with Jeffrey's mother, who had made the application. As a result, the British government had to change the law on corporal punishment in schools. This took some time to achieve, but corporal punishment was eventually abolished in most UK schools in 1987.

Human Rights Act 1998

In order to improve access to justice and the fairness of our laws and procedures, the *Human Rights Act 1998* was passed, incorporating into our law nearly all the rights contained in the Convention. Under this Act all our laws must, as far as possible, conform to the rights listed under the Convention, and public bodies – such as the armed forces, local authorities, schools, hospitals, the police, prisons and the courts – must carry out their work in a way that respects these basic human rights. If they don't, then the law or the actions of the public body can be challenged in our own courts. A statute that the courts say is "incompatible" with the rights in the Convention is capable of being changed quickly.

The Convention Rights in UK law

There are 16 basic rights in the Act. They go beyond matters of life and death, like freedom from torture and killing, extending to people's rights in everyday life: what they can say and do, their beliefs, their right to a fair trial and many other similar basic entitlements.

(Article 1 is introductory)

Article 2 Right to life

Everyone has the absolute right to have their life protected by law. There are only certain very limited circumstances where it is acceptable for the state to take away someone's life, e.g. if a police officer acts justifiably in self-defence. The *Human Rights Act* completely abolished the death penalty in the UK.

Article 3 Prohibition of torture

Everyone has the absolute right not to be tortured or subjected to treatment or punishment that is inhuman or degrading. The UK cannot deport someone to a country where they are likely to suffer torture or face the death penalty. .

Article 4 Prohibition of slavery and forced labour

Everyone has the absolute right not to be treated as a slave or forced to perform certain kinds of labour.

Article 5 Right to liberty and security

Everyone has the right not to be deprived of their liberty – 'arrested or detained' – except in limited cases specified in the Article (e.g. where they are suspected or convicted of committing a crime) and where this is justified by a clear legal procedure.

Article 6 Right to a fair trial

Everyone has the right to a fair and public hearing within a reasonable period of time. This applies to both civil and criminal proceedings. Hearings must be by an independent and impartial tribunal established by law. It is possible to exclude the public from the hearing (though not the judgment) in order to protect national security or public order. Anyone facing a criminal charge is presumed innocent until proved guilty according to law and has certain minimum guaranteed rights to defend themselves.

Article 7 No punishment without law

Everyone has the right to be protected from being found guilty of an offence if it wasn't against the law at the time it was committed. There is also protection against changes in the law which increase the possible sentence or the type of punishment for an offence.

Articles 8–11

The rights to freedoms in Articles 8-11 may be restricted where it is necessary to protect things like public health or safety, the rights of others, or to prevent crime. Interference with these rights that goes too far can be challenged in the courts who will try to strike a fair balance.

Article 8 Right to respect for private life

Everyone has the right to respect for their private and family life, their home and their correspondence.

Article 9 Freedom of thought, conscience and religion

Everyone is free to hold whatever views, beliefs and thoughts (including religious faith) they like.

Article 10 Freedom of expression

Everyone has the right to express their views on their own or in a group. This applies even if they are unpopular or disturbing. This right can be restricted in specified circumstances.

Article 11 Freedom of assembly and association

Everyone has the right to get together with other people in a peaceful way. They also have the right to associate with other people, which can include the right to form a trade union. These rights may be restricted only in specified circumstances.

Article 12 Right to marry

Men and women have the right to marry and start a family. Our national law still governs how and at what age this can take place.

(Article 13, which deals with legal remedies, is not incorporated into our law.)

Article 14 Prohibition of discrimination

Everyone has the right to benefit from these Convention rights regardless of race, religion, sex, political views or any other status, unless a restriction can be reasonably justified.

Article 1 of Protocol 1*
Protection of property

Everyone has the right to the peaceful enjoyment of their possessions. Public authorities cannot usually interfere with things we own or the way we use them, except in specified limited circumstances.

Article 2 of Protocol 1*
Right to education

Everyone has the right to access to the educational system.

Article 3 of Protocol 1*
Right to free elections

Elections must be free and fair, and take place by secret ballot. Some restrictions can be placed on those who are allowed to vote, e.g. by giving a minimum age.

Articles 1 and 2 of Protocol 13*
Abolition of the death penalty

These provisions abolish the death penalty.

*** (a 'protocol' is a later addition to the Convention)**

HOW DOES THE HUMAN RIGHTS ACT AFFECT US?

The Human Rights Act is a unique type of higher law, affecting all other laws. The rights and their limitations are a set of basic values. Respect for these rights and everything that goes with them may help change the way people think and behave. It is designed to create a society in which decisions and policies are better discussed and understood. But the freedoms protected by the Act are not a complete set of human values and do not, for example, include the right to work or freedom from poverty.

The Act cannot be used directly by one private individual against another. It is designed to indicate how judges in courts must interpret the law and how public bodies – such as the police, the prison service and local councils – must carry out their actions.

It protects fundamental freedoms – like liberty and free speech – but at the same time, allows limits to be placed on these rights in order to try to make sure that other people are also treated fairly.

For example, a person's right to liberty may be restricted if they are guilty of a serious crime. This is for other people's protection. Similarly there are limits placed on freedom of speech to prevent someone from shouting 'Fire!' in a crowded hall, when there isn't one.

voting and elections

Who can vote?

You must be 18 or over on the day of the election and your name must be on the electoral register maintained by your local council. For Parliamentary elections, you must be a national of the United Kingdom, the Commonwealth or of the Irish Republic, and either live in this country, or be a British citizen abroad but registered in the UK as an overseas voter. To vote for the Welsh Assembly you must also be on the electoral register in Wales. For European and local elections, nationals of the EU states living in the UK may also vote. The minimum voting age in the Isle of Man, Jersey and Guernsey is 16.

Who can't vote?

Those unable to vote in Parliamentary elections include most people compulsorily held for treatment for mental illness (although the rights of people in this category are not absolutely clear), most convicted prisoners, anyone convicted of corrupt practices at an election during the previous five years, and members of the House of Lords.

Registering to vote

You can register to vote at any time by contacting your local council election registration office or downloading a form from **www.aboutmyvote.co.uk**. An electoral registration form is also delivered before an election to every household in the country. The form should be completed with details of everyone living there, aged 16 and over. You're not automatically registered to vote, even if you pay Council Tax, so if you want to vote, you have to register. In any event, it is technically an offence to knowingly fail to put yourself on the electoral register.

You can check if your name is on the register of electors at your local electoral registration office.

Anyone can get a postal vote, provided that they are on the electoral register. There are also special arrangements for people who cannot get to the polling station on the day.

Methods are being considered to make the process of voting more up-to-date, including mobile polling stations and 'e-voting' through the internet, mobile phones and digital TV.

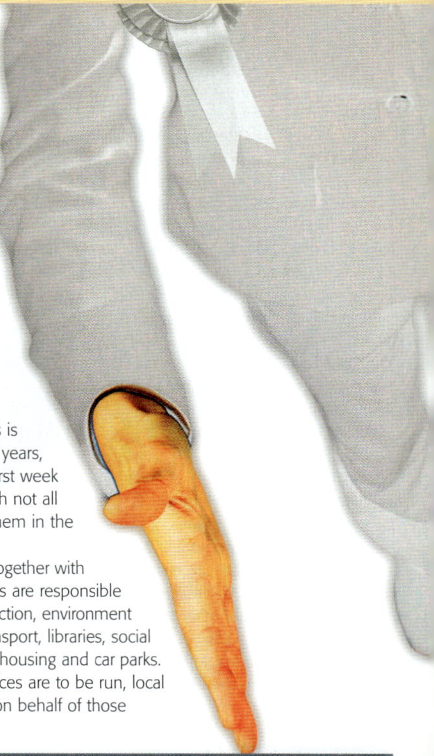

Who can you vote for?

Most people standing in local, national or European elections represent a political party. All political parties have to be registered with the Electoral Commission. The party will then select its candidates for each election. Some people stand as an independent without belonging to any political party.

Local elections

The election of local councillors is held every four years, usually in the first week of May, although not all councils hold them in the same year.

Between them, and sometimes together with national government, these councils are responsible for education, planning, refuse collection, environment and leisure services, passenger transport, libraries, social services, children's homes, council housing and car parks.

As well as deciding how the services are to be run, local councillors also take up problems on behalf of those living in their area.

LOCAL COUNCILLOR, AM, MP OR MEP?

Under the *Electoral Administration Act 2006*, you can now stand for political office from the age of 18. If you want to be a local councillor you must either:

- **have your name on the local electoral register; or**
- **rent (over the last twelve months) or own land or property in the area; or**
- **have worked or lived in the area for the last twelve months.**

These rules do not apply to Welsh Assembly members, MPs or MEPs. Candidates standing as an AM or MP must pay a deposit of £500, which they lose if they get less than 5% of the votes cast. The deposit for MEPs is £5,000. Deposits are not required in local council elections.

voting and elections

General elections

The election of all 646 MPs must take place at least every five years. Often, however, the party in power will call an election before this if it feels it will help its chances of gaining another term of office or, more rarely, because it has been defeated on a vital vote in the House of Commons or has lost the confidence of the House.

Almost all MPs represent a registered political party and each represents a defined area, called a constituency. The party with the greatest number of MPs forms the government, with the party leader becoming Prime Minister. If an MP dies or resigns, a by-election takes place to elect a new MP for the constituency.

Even if they are not a member of the Government, an MP can have influence by speaking in debates, talking to ministers and other MPs, and by trying to get a private member's Bill made law. MPs must represent everyone in their constituency.

Voting systems

Votes for general and by-elections in the United Kingdom are counted on a 'first past the post' system. People each cast one vote and the winning candidate is the one with the most votes. Elections to the European Parliament follow a different system, known as proportional representation, under which the number of seats each party receives is roughly equal to their share of the votes. Elections to the National Assembly for Wales use both systems. 40 Assembly Members are chosen using the 'first passed the post' system and 20 are chosen by proportional representation.

European elections

At European elections we elect members of the European Parliament that meets both in Strasbourg (France) and Brussels (Belgium). Elections take place every five years. Most candidates belong to one of the main political parties and, if elected, join the other MEPs from the other 26 countries in the European Union. The UK has 78 MEPs (out of a current total of 785). MEPs sit in multinational political groups with, for example, British Labour MEPs belonging to the Party of European Socialists, along with socialists from the other EU states.

MEPs help to make European law by examining and commenting on proposals made by the European Commission (see **european union,** pages 148–149).

Campaigning

If you feel strongly about something and want to get involved yourself, a library, Citizens Advice Bureau, or one of the organisations or websites listed in the **contacts** section can probably give you some of the information you need to make a start.

Campaigning can range from individual action to something more co-ordinated, as a member of a group. Letter writing is the usual starting point – do your research, send it to a named person (the most senior within the organisation), keep a copy, and try to get others involved as well. If you can get a letter published in a newspaper, many more will know about your views, but do give your name and address – although you can ask the paper not to publish it.

BRIEF CASE: NO MORE SECRECY

As part of its plan to introduce identity cards, the government drew up a report on the benefits and risks of the scheme. Lib Dem MP Mark Oaten asked to see a copy of the report, believing that this information should be publicly available. He was refused. The Liberal Democrat Party, which is against the introduction of identity cards, appealed against this decision – and was successful. In his ruling, the Information Commissioner stated that the report should be released because it was important for the public to have available information on the likely costs and benefits of identity cards.

Freedom of Information

Under the *Freedom of Information Act 2000*, anybody, regardless of their age, nationality or where they live, can ask for information from a public body in England, Wales and Northern Ireland. (Scotland has its own law.) A public body is any part of local or national government, including the National Health Service, police and schools.

You can ask a public body if they hold the information you are looking for, and if so, you are entitled to apply for that information.

Your request must:

- **be in writing;**
- **state clearly what information is required; and**
- **include your full name and address.**

The department or organisation must respond to your request as soon as possible, and within 20 working days. There may be a charge for this service. You will be told about this when you have made your application.

There are certain, specific reasons your request may be refused, for example for security reasons, or if the information is due to be published at a later date. See **contacts** for futher help and information.

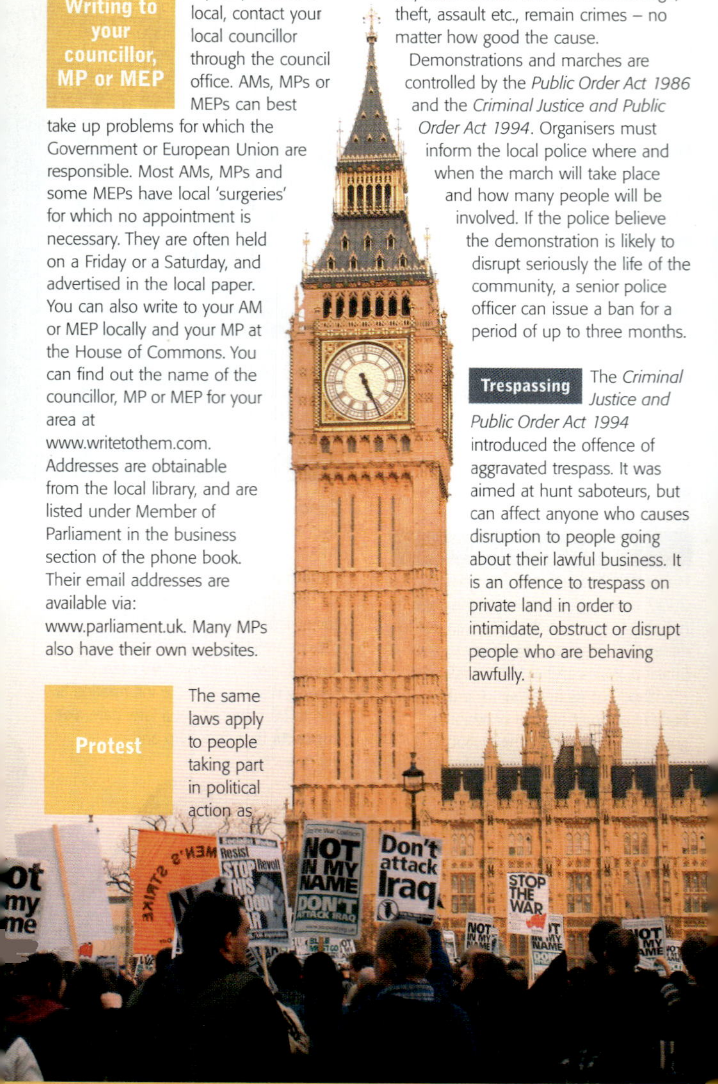

Writing to your councillor, MP or MEP

If your problem is local, contact your local councillor through the council office. AMs, MPs or MEPs can best take up problems for which the Government or European Union are responsible. Most AMs, MPs and some MEPs have local 'surgeries' for which no appointment is necessary. They are often held on a Friday or a Saturday, and advertised in the local paper. You can also write to your AM or MEP locally and your MP at the House of Commons. You can find out the name of the councillor, MP or MEP for your area at www.writetothem.com. Addresses are obtainable from the local library, and are listed under Member of Parliament in the business section of the phone book. Their email addresses are available via: www.parliament.uk. Many MPs also have their own websites.

Protest

The same laws apply to people taking part in political action as any other area of life. Criminal damage, theft, assault etc., remain crimes – no matter how good the cause.

Demonstrations and marches are controlled by the *Public Order Act 1986* and the *Criminal Justice and Public Order Act 1994*. Organisers must inform the local police where and when the march will take place and how many people will be involved. If the police believe the demonstration is likely to disrupt seriously the life of the community, a senior police officer can issue a ban for a period of up to three months.

Trespassing

The *Criminal Justice and Public Order Act 1994* introduced the offence of aggravated trespass. It was aimed at hunt saboteurs, but can affect anyone who causes disruption to people going about their lawful business. It is an offence to trespass on private land in order to intimidate, obstruct or disrupt people who are behaving lawfully.

Complaining

If you have a complaint about something you have bought or a service you have received, it's important to act quickly. Some companies, and many public services, have special procedures for dealing with complaints. If it's a public service, such as a hospital or benefits agency, you can ask to see a copy of their charter which shows the level of service you are entitled to expect. If your complaint is not dealt with properly, think about contacting your local councillor or MP, particularly if your problem is over a public service. Try to:

- **act as quickly as possible;**
- **think carefully about what you want to achieve and if necessary, get advice;**
- **make sure you talk or write directly to a person, such as the manager or director of services who has the authority to deal with your complaint;**
- **always find out the name of the person you are talking to;**
- **keep a record of phone calls or letters that you send;**
- **stick to the facts, and work out how the law can help you;**
- **state clearly what you want to be done, set a reasonable time within which this should happen, and get back in touch if they haven't met the deadline.**

Data protection

How can I check what they know about me?

If you are still unhappy with the way your problem has been handled, you may be able to take your case to an Ombudsman. See **contacts**, General.

People collect personal information about you all the time. Your school, your GP, the local council, shops, your mobile phone company, your bank, your employer, the police and many others all keep records on you. Sometimes it's facts like your age or how much you've spent on your mobile phone; sometimes it's opinions about say a health risk or whether you might commit an offence or fail an exam.

The *Data Protection Act 1998* says that this can be done as long as the people keeping and using the information follow various rules and regulations. The law tries to balance your right to privacy and fair treatment with other people's legitimate rights to keep and use information about you.

Very strict rules apply to other people collecting and using personal information such as your racial or ethnic origins, your political, religious, or other views, your sex life, any criminal offences and the state of your health. Usually your clear consent is needed before this information is stored or used.

One of the main protections you have is to be able to check what information is held about you and to get it put right if it's wrong.

You are known as a 'data subject' and the law says you can apply to anyone to ask if they hold information about you, and if so what it is, by making a 'subject access request'.

Applying for information You can write this in your own words, asking for all personal information held about you. Some organisations like the police have their own forms which you should use. You should identify yourself clearly and be as specific as possible about what you want to know. You can be asked to pay a fee. This is normally £10 but in some cases it can be as little as £2 (for credit information) or as much as £50 (for old handwritten medical records and some education records). You should get a reply within 40 days (or 15 school days if the request is to a school) – and in some cases shorter times must be met. If you think the information is wrong you can require that it is changed and if necessary go to court for an order to correct inaccurate information. Full details of your rights to check information held about you are available from The Information Commissioner's website – see **contacts**.

Judicial review If a public body – like a government department, local authority, or hospital – makes a decision which actually seems to be fundamentally unfair, you can apply to have that decision reviewed in the High Court. Known as judicial review, it's a way of having illegal or unreasonable decisions changed. Examples of this have been when people have challenged a ruling by the Home Office to deport someone who is a British citizen, or when they have questioned a hospital's right to withhold an operation in a genuinely urgent case.

A judicial review can normally be started only when all other avenues of complaint have been exhausted. It's a very complicated and expensive process and so, before doing anything, it's important to get advice from a solicitor who understands this area of law.

young citizen's **passport**

the european union

INDIVIDUALS ENGAGING IN SOCIETY

Citizenship Foundation

membership

Twenty-seven countries are currently members of the European Union (EU):

Austria, Belgium, Bulgaria, Cyprus, the Czech Republic, Denmark, Estonia, Finland, France, Germany, Greece, Hungary, Ireland, Italy, Latvia, Lithuania, Luxembourg, Malta, the Netherlands, Poland, Portugal, Romania, Slovakia, Slovenia, Spain, Sweden and the United Kingdom.

Membership negotiations have also taken place with Croatia, Macedonia and Turkey – but it is expected that further enlargement will be slower than in recent years.

Origins After the end of the Second World War, governments throughout Europe were determined not to repeat the horrors of the War, in which 50 million people had died.

Beginnings In 1951, France, Belgium, Italy, Luxembourg, the Netherlands, and West Germany signed an agreement setting up the European Coal and Steel Community through which the coal and steel production of all six countries came under the control of a single European authority.

The architects of this plan believed that placing coal and steel production outside the control of individual states would greatly reduce the likelihood of another war. Britain was invited to join the ECSC, but declined.

Growth In the early years co-operation was mainly designed to make it easier for member states to trade with one another. Gradually, the scope of the union has widened, and covers many areas today, including employment, the environment, transport, travel, foreign policy – and for 16 of the member states a common currency: the euro.

the single market

The idea of European states forming a single market has always been central to the development of the European Union.

A single market means that goods, services, people, and money must be able to move freely between member states.

Over the last 30 years member states have agreed all kinds of measures to make this possible:

- **taxes and duties on products have been made broadly similar between member states;**
- **technical and safety specifications of goods have been standardised, so that goods made in one state meet the standards required in another;**
- **people are allowed to travel, live, study, and work more-or-less wherever they wish.**

A single currency

The EU has also eased the movement of goods and people through the creation of a single currency, also sometimes called economic and monetary union (EMU).

The idea was first proposed in 1969, but the first significant steps were not taken until around 1990 when member states interested in moving towards a single currency began to prepare their economies for this process.

They were required to meet a number of conditions – usually described as convergence criteria – such as having low interest rates, keeping currency rates and prices stable and keeping government expenditure within certain limits.

the single market

The Euro

On 1 January 2002, after a transition period of two years, 12 of the then 15 EU member states moved to a single currency – the euro (€).

Today there are 16 countries where euro banknotes and coins are the only legal tender.

The seven euro notes, from €5–€500, are the same throughout the single currency area. Each country produces its own coins, of smaller value, although these can be used anywhere within the euro area, regardless of national origin.

Britain and the Euro

Britain, Denmark, and Sweden decided not to proceed with the single currency. Denmark voted against the euro in a referendum held in 2000, as did the people of Sweden in 2003. The British government has also undertaken to hold a referendum on the issue when the government believes that its own five convergence criteria have been met, but this is not likely to be in the near future.

travel and work

Measures have been gradually introduced to help people move around the EU as easily as possible.

Travel

Citizens of an EU member state have the right to travel to any EU country, if they have a valid passport or identity card. This right may be restricted only for reasons of public order, public security, or public health.

EU citizens also have the right to travel within the EU with members of their family, but if they do not have EU nationality they may be required to have a visa, in addition to their passport.

Border controls

There are no customs checks for people travelling from one EU member state to another – although police controls on some frontiers remain, checking for terrorist activity, drug-trafficking and organised crime.

In addition, identity checks for EU citizens have been abolished at many borders under what is called the Schengen Agreement. This allows people to travel from one country to another without having their passport or identity documents examined. Twenty-four member states, not including Britain and Ireland, have joined the group.

Health care

Citizens of EU member states who fall ill within another EU country are entitled to emergency treatment under that country's health scheme.

The treatment is either free, or its cost is reduced for someone from Britain who can show the medical authorities their European Health Insurance Card (see **travel**, page 102). A person who does not have an EHIC is still entitled to treatment, but may be asked to pay its full cost.

Help

An EU citizen who gets into difficulties in a country outside the EU may seek protection from the embassy or consulate of any EU member state.

For example, a British student arrested in a Russian city without a British consular office is entitled to help from the Swedish or Finnish consulate. For emergency services in any EU state, dial 112.

Work

British citizens are entitled to work in any EU country, and should be offered employment under the same conditions as citizens of that state. It would be against the law, for example, for an Italian firm to require British job applicants to have higher qualifications than their Italian counterparts – and vice versa.

Most jobs are open to all EU citizens. However, member states are allowed to insist that only nationals of that state hold certain public service posts, such as those in the police or armed forces.

A residence permit is required for anyone who wants to stay in another member state for more than three months. This requires ID, if they don't have a paid job, and evidence of financial support.

Conditions Generally speaking, a British citizen working in another EU member state has exactly the same employment rights and duties as everyone else in that country, and it is against the law for that person to be discriminated against on grounds of their nationality.

A British worker in Berlin, for example, should receive the same pay, employment opportunities, and health and safety protection as his or her German counterparts.

Qualifications EU citizens who are qualified to work in a particular profession in their own country are also able to carry out that work in any other member state. However not all qualifications are automatically recognised – and applicants might need to check if their particular diploma or certificate is recognised.

Benefits Citizens of EU member states are entitled to the same welfare and social security benefits as nationals of the country in which they are working. This covers sickness and maternity benefits, benefits for accidents at work and unemployment. They also have the same rights, (where it is available), to accommodation, such as local authority housing.

Taxes A person who lives and works in an EU member state must normally pay taxes in the same way as any other resident of that country. Levels of taxation vary from one EU state to another, but work is under way to try to find ways of harmonising taxation across member states.

goods

Customs duties

Generally speaking, goods purchased by people for their own use may be bought in other member states and brought back to Britain without having to pay extra tax or duties. People can bring in as much tobacco and alcohol from other EU member states as they like, as long as it is for personal use only and not for resale. But there is a limit of 200 cigarettes if travelling from Bulgaria, Estonia, Latvia, Lithuania, and Romania. Customs officials in the UK have the right to stop people and check this, and to confiscate any items they believe are not for personal use.

governing europe

The structure of the government of the European Union is not easy to understand – possibly because there are several organisations that help to determine EU policy.

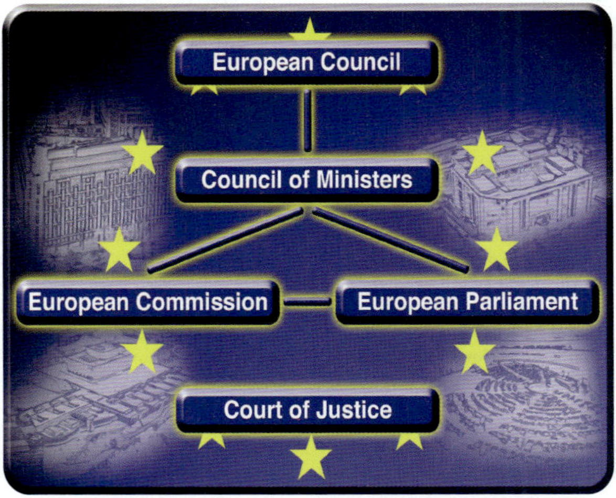

THE EUROPEAN COUNCIL

The European Council is the name given to the regular meetings between the heads of the member states. They decide the issues the European Union should be concerned with. In the past this has included unemployment, drug trafficking, and enlarging the EU.

The Council of Ministers

The Council of Ministers is one of the most influential bodies in the EU. It consists of government ministers from each member state with powers to take decisions about how the EU is run, decide policy, and negotiate with non-member states on behalf of the EU. It's at the centre of government in the EU, rather like the Cabinet is in Britain.

Decisions

Until the mid 1980s, decisions by the Council of Ministers tended to have to be unanimous. If a nation disagreed, the measure could not be passed. Today the Council generally uses a system called qualified majority voting. Each member state has a certain number of votes, broadly reflecting the size of the country in terms of its population.

For example, France, Germany, Italy, and the United Kingdom have 29 votes. Smaller countries, like Cyprus and Latvia, have four.

The European Commission

Based in Brussels, the European Commission is rather like the civil service of the European Union, taking care of the day-to-day running of the organisation. About 25,000 people work for the Commission, making it one of Europe's largest institutions. The Commission does several different jobs. It:

- **drafts proposals for new EU laws or policies;**
- **checks that EU laws and treaties are properly applied;**
- **begins legal action against member states or businesses that it believes are not following EU law;**
- **represents the EU on the international stage.**

EU Commissioners Each member state appoints one commissioner to take responsibility for running one particular aspect of EU business.

There are 27 commissioners in all. The current President, José Manuel Barroso, is from Portugal, and former leader of the House of Lords and Lord President of the Council, Catherine Ashton, is the UK representative. Currently she is EU Commissioner for Trade.

Changes to the EU

A draft EU Constitution was agreed by EU leaders in 2004 as a way of modernising the EU. It had to be approved by every EU country through either Parliament or a referendum, but in 2005 was rejected by France and the Netherlands. The idea of adopting the EU Constitution has now been dropped and in 2007 a new Reform Treaty was proposed instead. This, known as the Lisbon Treaty, was signed in December 2007, and will carry out a number of reforms previously proposed in the EU Constitution. The Treaty was supposed to come into force in January 2009, but has been challenged by a number of member states, making it unclear when it will be adopted.

The European Parliament The European Parliament currently consists of 785 MEPs (Members of the European Parliament). The Parliament meets in Brussels, Luxembourg and Strasbourg.

In the course of a month, MEPs usually meet for one week in Strasbourg, and for two weeks, on committee work, in Brussels. Parliamentary support staff are based in Brussels and Luxembourg.

Powers Today, MEPs:

- **decide, together with the Council of Ministers, on EU law;**
- **control more than half the money that the EU spends;**
- **watch over the European Commission and approve the appointment of all Commissioners.**

Elections The UK is allocated 72 of the 785 seats in the European Parliament. At the last election in 2004, the Conservatives were the largest UK party in the European Parliament.

Voting In the UK, as in all other EU member states, voting in European Parliamentary elections is open to any EU citizen, provided they are on the local register of electors.

Contact Debates in the European Parliament are open to the public, and groups and individuals can visit the Parliamentary building. MEPs may be reached by e-mail or by post or phone at their constituency office.

Petitions All EU citizens have the right to submit a petition to the President of the European Parliament, Hans-Gert Pöttering (the address is Rue Wiertz, B-1047, Brussels) or online, giving their view on a matter that is within the remit of the EU. The petition can be in any form, as long as it contains the sender's name, address, occupation, and signature.

BRIEF CASE

In 1999, the European Parliament ordered an investigation into fraud and corruption by members of the European Commission. The report of the investigation was very critical of the Commission and led to all 20 Commissioners resigning.

BRIEF CASE

Following a recent successful petition to the EU, the Greek authorities are now required to admit EU citizens to their museums under the same conditions as Greek nationals.

law makers

Today in Britain, MPs and judges still create and shape the law in much the same way as they have done for several hundred years. See law, government and human rights, pages 128–129.

However, our membership of the European Union requires all our laws to follow the treaties and agreements that we have made as members of the EU.

In this sense, European law has become the most important source of law in Britain. This is not to say that all our law comes from Europe, but it does mean that all our current and future laws must not break the principles set out in the treaties that we have signed.

BRIEF CASE: Patricia

In 1994, British courts heard the case of Patricia Day, who was made redundant after working for nearly five years as a part-time cleaner. Her employer, Hertfordshire County Council, stated that under UK law she was not entitled to any redundancy pay because she worked for less than 16 hours a week.

The judges decided that, although this practice did not break UK law, it was a form of discrimination against women, as most of the part-time workforce was female.

As sex discrimination in employment was expressly forbidden in European Union law, the British government had to change the law. Shortly afterwards the law was altered to give full and part-time workers similar employment rights.

The European Union

Law created through our membership of the European Union normally reaches us in four ways – through treaties, regulations, directives, and court judgments.

Treaties

Treaties are agreements made between our government and other EU member states, which become incorporated into our law by Parliament. Treaties often contain broad agreements on which further action will be based. Sometimes, however, they include sections that can have a very specific effect on people's lives.

BRIEF CASE

The Treaty of Rome, signed in 1957, is the agreement upon which the European Economic Community was established. Article 119 of the Treaty states that men and women should receive equal pay for equal work.

Regulations Regulations are the laws that put treaties into practice. Regulations automatically have effect in the UK, and no new national law is required.

BRIEF CASE

An important section of the Treaty of Rome says that people should be able to move freely for work between member states. The regulations that have followed the Treaty require member states to introduce new laws to ensure this works. As a result, all member states needed to have laws granting visiting EU workers the same rights to education and housing as the citizens of their own state.

Directives Directives, like regulations, are a means of putting an EU objective into practice, but member states are able to choose for themselves how this will be done.

BRIEF CASE

In 2001, the EU issued a directive requiring companies operating in the EU to inform employees about any decision affecting their jobs – especially if it might lead to redundancy. This directive was made following a number of unexpected redundancies in France, made by several multi-national companies. The UK was given seven years in which to implement the directive.

Court judgments The European Court of Justice considers all matters of European Community law. Located in Luxembourg, it is the most senior court in Europe and overrules all national courts. Member states must follow its decisions.

BRIEF CASE: John

Until recently, UK winter fuel payments were paid to women from the age of 60, but not to men until they reached 65. This was challenged in the UK courts by retired postman John Taylor, who claimed it was unlawful discrimination. The British High Court asked the European Court of Justice to deliver a judgement on this in the light of European Community law. The European Court announced that this practice did not follow Community law and that winter fuel payments should be given to men and women under the same terms.

Getting information & advice

- **Before you write, phone or ask for information, think carefully about exactly what you need to know.**
- **Don't be overlong in your explanation, keep to the most important details.**
- **If you are telephoning, you will probably first speak to a receptionist who may not be able to answer your question. Explain that you'd like to talk to someone about... (name the subject), & you should be put through. If they can't help, they may be able to give you the name of someone who can.**
- **It sometimes helps to put a few key words down on paper to remind you of what you want to say. You may also need a pen & paper to make a note of what you are told.**
- **It's a good idea to ask who you are talking to so, if you write or phone again, you will know the name of the person you first spoke to.**

The following organisations are arranged according to the chapters in the main part of the book & are just a few of the many that exist to help with the whole range of law-related problems.

General

Childline, Freepost NATN 1111, London E1 6BR, **www.childline.org.uk**, offers a free 24hr helpline for any child in danger or distress, tel 0800 1111, also free on most mobile networks. If you live away from home (eg in a foster or care home, or at boarding school) there is a special helpline, tel 0800 88 44 44, open 3.30pm-9.30pm, weekdays, & 2.00pm-8.00pm, weekends.

Children's Legal Centre, University of Essex, Wivenhoe Park, Colchester, Essex CO4 3SQ, provides free independent legal advice to children & their parents or carers. Call 0800 783 2187 for immediate advice & guidance; the child law advice line is 0845 120 2948: both Mon-Fri, 9.00am-5.00pm, **www.childrenslegalcentre.com**

Citizens Advice Bureau, usually known as the CAB, gives free, confidential & independent information & advice on all kinds of problems. You can enquire by phone or at one of their offices in most towns & cities. For your nearest CAB, see the local phone book. Also see **www.adviceguide.org.uk**, for information on a wide range of many topics, available in several languages.

Community Legal Advice, provides free information on legal services to those eligible for legal aid (eg on low income &/or benefits), tel 0845 345 4 345, Mon-Fri, 9.00am-6.30pm, **www.clsdirect.org.uk**.

Directgov is a website with information on a wide range of subjects, including law, employment, education, benefits & driving - plus details of public services, local & national government, **www.direct.gov.uk**

Disability Law Services, Ground Floor, 39-45 Cavell Street, London E1 2BP, tel 020 7791 9800, open Mon-Fri, 10.00am-1.00pm, 2.00pm-5.00pm. Free legal advice for disabled people on disability discrimination, benefits, education, employment, consumer issues & community care, **www.dls.org.uk**.

Free Representation Unit, 6th floor, 289-293 High Holborn, London WC1V 7HZ; a network of barristers & law students who represent clients without charge at social security & employment tribunals. They only take cases referred to them by solicitors, law centres & CABs, mainly in SE England. **www.freerepresentationunit.org.uk**.

Law Centres Federation, 293-299 Kentish Town Road, London NW5 2TJ. tel 020 7428 4400. The website, **www.lawcentres.org.uk**, gives the name & address of your nearest Law Centre where free or low cost legal advice can be obtained.

Law Society, 113 Chancery Lane, London WC2A 1PL, tel 020 7242 1222; in Wales, Capital Tower, Greyfriars Road, Cardiff, CF10 3AG, tel 029 2064 5254. The Law Society does not give legal advice, but can provide information on finding & using a solicitor, & how to complain if you are dissatisfied with a solicitor's standard of service, **www.lawsociety.org.uk**

Liberty, 21 Tabard Street, London SE1 4LA, tel 020 7403 3888, a campaigning organisation dealing mainly with human rights. An advice line is open on Mon & Thurs, 6.30pm-8.30pm, Wed 12.30pm-2.30pm, tel 0845 123 2307, or 0203 145 0461, **www.liberty-human-rights.org.uk**. Liberty's other website, **www.yourrights.org.uk**, provides further information on human rights & the law.

National Youth Agency, Eastgate House, 19-23 Humberstone Road, Leicester LE5 3GJ, tel 0116 242 7350 provides an online information resource, **www.youthinformation.com**, with self-help information about many of the topics covered in this book.

The Ombudsman, if you have a problem with your local authority, a government department, the health service, an insurance company, a bank or building society or a legal service, & are not happy with how your complaint has been dealt with, you can refer your case to the relevant Ombudsman. You must first, however, have done everything you can to sort things out yourself with the person or organisation concerned. Your local CAB can explain how to submit a complaint, or you can find the ombudsman you require from the British & Irish Ombudsman Association, **www.bioa.org.uk**. If the Ombudsman decides your complaint is easonable, the organisation responsible will be sked to do something about it. This could mean hat you get an apology or compensation, or hat new procedures are put into place, so the ame thing doesn't happen again.

heSite.org, YouthNet UK, 50 Featherstone treet, London EC1 8RT, tel 020 7250 5700, ives details on a wide range of topics, ncluding the law, aimed mainly at 16-24 year-lds, **www.thesite.org.uk**.

outh Access, 1-2 Taylor's Yard, 67 Alderbrook Road, London SW12 8AD, tel 020 8772 9900. f you have a problem you would like to discuss confidentially, Youth Access can put you in touch with someone locally who may be able to help. There is no charge. Your local Youth Access agency can be found via "Directory of Services" on the Youth Access website, **www.youthaccess.org.uk**.

Life

SEX, CONTRACEPTION, PREGNANCY AND ABORTION

AFLaGA, BCM Box 8431, London WC1N 3XX, gives advice & support to serving & ex-serving members of the armed forces who are lesbian or gay. The helpline, tel 0870 740 7755, operates Wed 7.00-9.00pm & Sun 9.00am-7.00pm, but messages can also be left outside this time, **www.aflaga.org.uk**. The website, **www.proud2serve.net**, provides further information for those who want to find out more about the background to being gay in the military, & the military & civil law that covers this.

British Association for Adoption & Fostering, Saffron House, 6-10 Kirby Street, London EC1N 8TS, tel 020 7421 2600; in Wales, 7 Cleeve House, Lambourne Crescent, Cardiff, CF14 5GP, tel, 029 2076 1155. BAAF offers advice and information on adoption and fostering, in addition to working for children who may have become separated from their birth families, **www.baaf.org.uk**.

British Pregnancy & Advisory Service, 20 Timothy's Bridge Road, Stratford Enterprise Park, Stratford-upon-Avon, CV37 9BF, tel 0845 365 5050, has 56 consultation centres and clinics throughout the UK providing pregnancy tests, consultation, emergency contraception & abortions. Appointments available via BPAS's Actionline, tel 08457 30 40 30, Mon-Fri 8.00am-9.00pm, Saturday 8.30am-6.00pm, Sunday, 9.30am-2.30pm, **www.bpas.org**.

Brook Advisory Centres, 421 Highgate Studios, 53-79 Highgate Road, London NW5 1TL, tel, 020 7284 6040, offer free & confidential advice & counselling on sex & contraception for young people under 25. There are 17 Centres throughout the UK. Two advice lines (both free) are open Mon- Fri 9.00am-5.00pm, 0800 0185 023 and 0808 802 1234., There is a 24hr helpline on sexual health, tel 020 7950 7700. If you are 19 or under, you can call *Sexwise* (**www.ruthinking.co.uk**) from 7.00am-12 midnight (daily) on 0800 28 29 30, anonymity guaranteed, **www.brook.org.uk**.

Fpa, 50 Featherstone Street, London EC1Y 8QU, tel 020 7608 5240, provides detailed information on contraception & sexual health; in Wales, Suite D1, Canton House, 435-451 Cowbridge Road East, Cardiff CF5 1JH, tel 029 2064 4034. The helpline, for advice about pregnancy, abortion, sexually transmitted diseases & sexual wellbeing, is available, Mon-Fri 9.00am-6.00pm, tel 0845 122 8690. A 24hr sexual health helpline is available for information on HIV, AIDS, local clinics & support services, tel 0800 567 123. **www.fpa.org.uk**

Marie Stopes International UK, 1 Conway Street, Fitzroy Square, London W1T 6LP, tel 020 7636 6200, offers information on contraception, abortion, sexual health & other services. For appointments, details of UK centres & information leaflets, tel 0845 300 8090 (24hr), **www.mariestopes.org.uk**.

Stonewall, Tower Building, York Road, London SE1 7NX, offers information & advice for lesbians, gay men & bisexuals, tel (free) 08000 50 20 20, Mon-Fri 9.30am-5.30pm. **www.stonewall.org.uk**. In Wales, 3rd Floor, Transport House, 1 Cathedral Road, Cardiff, CF11 9SB, tel 029 2023 7744.

HIV & AIDS

Avert, 4 Brighton Road, Horsham, West Sussex RH13 5BA, tel 01403 210 202, an international HIV & AIDS charity base in the UK. The website gives details of local UK community organisations & clinics where advice & help are available. **www.avert.org/aidsuk.htm**.

National AIDS Helpline, a 24hr freephone service, staffed by advisors who can deal with questions on sex, drugs or relationships, tel 0800 567 123. Welsh & other language options are available.

NAZ Project London, Palingswick House, 241 King Street, London W6 9LP, tel 020 8741 1879, providing advice & support on HIV, AIDS & sexual health, targeted at black & minority ethnic communities in London, **www.naz.org.uk**.

Positively Women, 347-349 City Road, London EC1V 1LR, tel 020 7713 0444, able to provide practical & emotional support for women with HIV & AIDS, & their families, helpline tel 020 7713 0222, (will call back free of charge), Mon-Fri 10.00am-1.00pm, 2.00pm-4.00pm, **www.positivelywomen.org.uk**.

Terrence Higgins Trust, 314-320 Gray's Inn Road, London WC1X 8DP, tel, 020 7812 1600, provides support & information for people affect with & by HIV & AIDS. For the THT Direct Helpline, tel 0845 1221 200, Mon-Fri 10.00am-

10.00pm, Sat-Sun 12noon-6.00pm, **www.tht.org.uk**. See website also for details of ways to arrange for an HIV test.

DRUGS & ADDICTION

Alcohol Concern, 64 Leman Street, London E1 8EU, tel, 020 7264 0510, provides information, but not advice (see Drinkline, below), on alcohol problems, **www.alcoholconcern.org.uk**

Drinkaware, 7-10 Chandos Street, London W1G 9DQ, tel, 020 7307 7450, provides practical advice and information about all aspects of alcohol consumption, **www.drinkaware.co.uk**.

Drinkline, a 24hr confidential advice & helpline for those with drink-related concerns, tel 0800 917 82 82.

Drugaid, MIDAS, 2nd Floor, Oldway House, Castle Street, Merthyr Tydfil CF47 8UX, tel 01685 721991, & also 16 Clive St, Caerphilly, Mid Glamorgan CF83 1GE, tel 029 2086 8675 (for alcohol related concerns), or 08700 600 310 (for drug related concerns) offer counselling, support & information for drug & alcohol users, their friends & family in South Wales, Mon-Fri, 9.00am-5.00pm. **www.drugaidcymru.com**

DrugScope, Prince Consort House, Suite 204 (2nd Floor), 109/111 Farringdon Road, London, EC1R 3BW, tel, 020 7520 7550, for information about drug advice agencies in your area. In Wales there is a 24 hour, free bilingual drugs & alcohol helpline, tel 0800 6 33 55 88, **www.drugscope.org.uk**

FRANK, a website, **www.talktofrank.com**, & 24hr free confidential helpline providing advice & information on all types of drug taking - for drug users, their family & friends, tel 0800 77 66 00.

Narcotics Anonymous (NA),202 City Road, London, EC1V 2PH, 020 7251 4007, operates a 24hr, seven-day confidential helpline, tel 0845 373 3366 (or 020 7730 0009, Mon-Fri, 10am-10pm), for those trying to recover from addiction, their friends & family. See website for local NA groups, **www.ukna.org**.

Release, 388 Old Street, London EC1V 9LT, tel, 020 7749 4044, for information & legal advice on drug-related problems, the law & human rights. A helpline, tel 0845 4500 215, is open Mon-Fri 11.00am-1.00pm, 2.00pm-4.00pm (leave a message outside these hours and Release will call you back within 24 hours), **www.release.org.uk**.

HEALTH

Community Health Councils in Wales give advice to anyone who has a complaint about any aspect of the health services; find under 'C' in the phone book.

MIND, PO Box 277, Manchester, M60 3XN, & Mind Cymru, 3rd Floor, Quebec House, Castlebridge, Cowbridge Road East, Cardiff CF11 9AB, tel. 029 2039 5123, the leading mental health charity in England & Wales providing information on all aspects of mental health. Infoline, tel 0845 766 0163, Mon-Fri 9.00am-5.00pm, **www.mind.org.uk**.

NHS Direct, a 24hr helpline providing confidential advice to anyone concerned about their health, or with questions about any aspect of the Health Service, tel 0845 4647, **www.nhsdirect.nhs.uk**.

Samaritans, talk to anyone feeling desperate, lonely or suicidal. You can say what you like, you need not give your name; it's entirely confidential. They can be reached by phone at any time, every day of the year. The central number is 08457 90 90 90. For your local branch, use the website or look under 'S' in the phone book; many offer drop-in personal support, **www.samaritans.org.uk**.

Sane, 1st Floor, Cityside House, 40 Adler Street, London E1 1EE, tel 020 7375 1002, able to provide information & advice to anyone (including friends & family) suffering from mental health problems. They can put you in touch with support available in your local area. A helpline operates 6.00pm-11.00pm, every day of the year, tel 0845 767 8000, **www.sane.org.uk**.

Safety

PERSONAL SAFETY

Equality & Human Rights Commission, 3 More London, Riverside, Tooley Street, London, SE1 2RG, tel, 020 3117 0235; also Arndale House, The Arndale Centre, Manchester, M4 3AQ, tel, 0161 829 8100; in Wales, 3rd Floor, 3 Callaghan Square, Cardiff, CF10 5BT, tel, 029 2044 7710, is an independent working to eliminate unfair discrimination. Information and guidance on discrimination and human rights is available via its helplines: in England, tel, 0845 604 6610; in Wales, tel 0845 604 8810. Lines are open from 9.00am-5.00pm on Mon, Tue, Thu and Fri, and from 9.00am-8.00pm on Wed, **www.equalityhumanrights.com**

Rape Crisis (England & Wales) runs Rape Crisis Support Groups, throughout Britain, offering free & confidential advice to any woman or girl who has been raped or sexually assaulted. These groups also provide information on support agencies for men, **www.rapecrisis.org.uk**.

Survivors UK, 12A Evelyn Court, Grinstead Road, London, SE8 5AD, tel, 020 8691 8236. A helpline, open Mon, Tues & Thurs, 7.00pm-10.00pm, tel 0845 122 1201, gives advice & information to men who are victims of sexual violence or abuse, **www.survivorsuk.org**.

zy Lamplugh Trust, National Centre for rsonal Safety, Hampton House, 20 Albert mbankment, London SE1 7TJ, tel 020 7091 014, open 9.00am-5.00pm, Mon-Fri, gives formation, guidance, training & resources on ersonal safety (including an online personal afety shop), **www.suzylamplugh.org**. The rust's website aimed at young people is at **www.livelifesafe.org.uk**.

VICTIMS & COMPENSATION

The Court Service publishes information for victims of crime & details of local courts, available from HMCS Headquarters, Customer Service Unit, 4th Floor, 102 Petty France, London SW1H 9AJ, **www.hmcourts-service.gov.uk**.

Criminal Injuries Compensation Authority, ay House, 300 Bath Street, Glasgow G2 4LN, rovides compensation for victims of crimes of iolence. Information & application forms vailable by post, phone, tel 0800 358 3601 Mon-Fri 8.30am-6.00pm, Sat 9.30am-1.00pm) r via the website, **www.cica.gov.uk**.

Victim Support, Hallam House, 50-60 Hallam Street, London, W1W 6JL, tel, 020 7268 0200; n Wales, Victim Support, 1a Victoria Park Road, Cardiff, CF5 1EZ, tel, 02920 56 90 59. Victim Support runs a helpline providing support to people who have been victims of, or witnesses o, a crime. The Victim Support helpline, tel 0845 30 30 900, is open Mon-Fri 9.00am-9.00pm, Sat-Sun 9.00am-7.00pm & 9.00am-5.00pm bank holidays, **www.victimsupport.com**.

Education

The Advisory Centre for Education (ACE), Unit 1c Aberdeen Studios, 22 Highbury Grove, London N5 2DQ, offers information & free telephone advice on many subjects including exclusion, bullying, special educational needs & school admission, tel 0808 800 5793, Mon-Fri 10.00am-5.00pm. An exclusion information line is open 24hrs, tel 020 7704 9822, **www.ace-ed.org.uk**.

Children's Legal Centre, University of Essex, Wivenhoe Park, Colchester, Essex CO4 3SQ, offers information on education law, tel 0845 120 2948, Mon-Fri,9.00am-5.00pm, **www.childrenslegalcentre.com**.

Department for Children, Schools & Families, Sanctuary Buildings, Great Smith Street, London, SW1P 3BT. Public Enquiry Unit, tel 0870 000 2288, Mon-Fri, 9.00am-5.00pm, for information about legal & other aspects of education, **www.dcsf.gov.uk**.

Education Otherwise, PO Box 325, Kings Lynn PE34 3XW, provides information & advice for people choosing to educate their children out of school, tel 0845 478 6345, **www.education-otherwise.org**

Independent Schools Council, St Vincent House, 30 Orange Street, London WC2H 7HH, tel 020 7766 7070, for information on education in the independent sector, **www.isc.co.uk**.

Work and training

ACAS (the Advisory, Conciliation & Arbitration Service), Brandon House, 180 Borough High Street, London SE1 1LW, runs a helpline giving information on a wide range of employment issues, open Mon-Fri 8.00am-6.00pm, tel 08457 47 47 47. Details of regional offices given on website, **www.acas.org.uk**.

Department for Children, Schools & Families, Public Enquiry Unit, tel 0870 000 2288. for information on legal & other aspects of education, **www.dcsf.gov.uk**.

Equality & Human Rights Commission, 3 More London, Riverside, Tooley Street, London, SE1 2RG, tel, 020 3117 0235; also Arndale House, The Arndale Centre, Manchester, M4 3AQ, tel, 0161 829 8100; in Wales, 3rd Floor, 3 Callaghan Square, Cardiff, CF10 5BT, tel, 029 2044 7710, is an independent working to eliminate unfair discrimination. Information and guidance on discrimination and human rights is available via its helplines: in England, tel, 0845 604 6610; in Wales, tel 0845 604 8810. Lines are open from 9.00am-5.00pm on Mon, Tue, Thu and Fri, and from 9.00am-8.00pm on Wed, **www.equalityhumanrights.com**

Health & Safety Executive (HSE), Rose Court, 2 Southwark Bridge, London, SE1 9HS is responsible for checking health & safety at work throughout England & Wales. They can send information explaining the law & can tell you whom to contact if you have a health & safety problem. The HSE Infoline is open Mon-Fri, 8.30am-6.00pm, tel 0845 345 0055, **www.hse.gov.uk**.

The National Minimum Wage Helpline, Freepost PHQ1 Newcastle-upon-Tyne, NE98 1ZH, provides information about the National Minimum Wage for people of all ages. Can also be used to make a complaint about an employer who is suspected of not paying the minimum wage, tel 0845 6000 678, Mon-Fri, 9.00am-5.00pm, **www.hmrc.gov.uk/nmw**

Money

Association of British Insurers, Consumer Information Dept., 51 Gresham Street, London EC2V 7HQ, tel 020 7600 3333, for leaflets & information on insurance, **www.abi.org.uk**.

Benefits, information is available from your local Jobcentre Plus office, listed in the phone book, & from **www.dwp.gov.uk**, & **www.jobcentreplus.gov.uk**

Consumerdirect, is a telephone & online consumer advice service, providing information on consumer problems, legal rights & how to complain, tel 08454 04 05 06, open Mon-Fri 8.00am-6.30pm, Sat 9.00am-1.00pm. For Welsh language service, tel 08454 04 05 05, **www.consumerdirect.gov.uk**.

HM Revenue & Customs, for free information leaflets & general enquiries contact any HMRC enquiry centre, see **www.hmrc.gov.uk**, or your local phone book. For a self-assessment form, tel 0845 9000 404, 8.00am-8.00pm every day, including weekends & bank holidays. If you are not a taxpayer & want to claim back tax paid on deposits (bank, building society etc), tel 0845 9890 0645 Mon-Thu 8.30am-5.00pm, Fri 8.30am-4.30pm.

National Debtline, Tricorn House, 51-53 Hagley Road, Edgbaston, Birmingham B16 8TP, for confidential help with debt problems & advice pack, tel 0808 808 4000 (Mon-Fri 9.00am-9.00pm, Sat 9.30am-1.00pm), **www.nationaldebtline.co.uk**.

PhonepayPlus (previously ICSTIS), Clove Building, 4 Maguire Street, London SE1 2NQ, is an organisation that regulates products or services that are charged to users' phone bills or pre-pay accounts. Their role is to respond to questions and complaints about premium rate phone services like helplines, news alerts, interactive games etc. If you have a complaint about any of these services, complete an online form, or phone (free) 0800 500 212, Mon-Fri, 8.00am-6.00pm for information or advice, **www.phonepayplus.org.uk**

Trading Standards Offices are in almost every town & city, & give free advice on a wide range of consumer problems. The address of your local office will be in the phone book, under 'T', or available from your local county or borough council or from **www.tradingstandards.gov.uk**.

Family

British Association for Adoption & Fostering, Saffron House, 6-10 Kirby Street, London EC1N 8TS, tel 020 7421 2600; and in Wales, 7 Cleeve House, Lambourne Crescent, Cardiff, CF14 5GP, tel, 029 2076 1155 & 19 Bedford Street, Rhyl, LL18 1SY, tel, 01745 336 336, provides advice & information for those thinking of adopting or fostering, or tracing their birth parents, **www.baaf.org.uk**.

Cafcass (Children & Family Court Advisory & Support Service), 6th Floor, Sanctuary Buildings, Great Smith Street, London SW1P 3BT, tel, 0844 353 3350; in Wales, Bromfield House, Queens Lane, Mold, Flintshire,CH7 1XB, tel, 01352 744537/744538, with local offices throughout England and Wales, looks after the interests of children involved in family proceedings in court, eg divorce, adoption, care or supervision, **www.cafcass.gov.uk**

Carers UK, 20 Great Dover Street, London,SE1 4LX, tel, 020 7378 4999, **www.carersuk.org** In Wales, Carers Wales, River House, Ynysbridge Court, Gwaelod y Garth, Cardiff CF15 9SS, tel 029 2081 1370, **www.carerswales.org**, works to help all carers, including young people. For personal help, contact Carersline, tel (free) 0808 808 7777, Wed & Thurs, 10.00am-12noon, 2.00pm-4.00pm.

Childline, Freepost NATN 1111, London E1 6BR, **www.childline.org.uk**, offers a free 24hr helpline for any child in danger or distress, tel 0800 1111, also free on most mobile networks. If you live away from home (eg in a foster or care home, or at boarding school) there is a special helpline, tel 0800 88 44 44, open 3.30pm-9.30pm, weekdays, & 2.00pm-8.00pm, weekends.

Kidscape, 2 Grosvenor Gardens, London SW1W 0DH, tel 020 7730 3300, provides free information & advice to children, their parents/carers & those who work with them, on bullying & abuse & keeping safe. A helpline, tel 08451 205 204, is available Mon, Tue 10.00am-8.00pm, Wed-Fri, 10.00am-4.00pm, primarily for parents of children who are being bullied, **www.kidscape.org.uk**.

Law Society Children Panel. The Law Society website has a list of solicitors who can advise & represent you in matters concerning parental & other family relationships, **www.lawsociety.org.uk**.

Missing People is a confidential service allowing someone who has run away from home, to leave a message for family & friends to let them know they are alive & well, **www.missingpeople.org.uk** The Missing People's adult service - Message Home service for those over the age of 18 is available on (freephone) 0800 700 740, or via email, messagehome@missingpeople.org.uk The Runaway Helpline is a national confidential service for anyone who has run away from home or care, or has been forced to leave home. Information or help is available on (freephone) 0808 800 7070, or email runaway@missingpeople.org.uk

National Missing People Helpline, tel 0500 700 700 (free, 24hrs) provides help, information & advice to families of missing people. Phone the same number if you have information about a missing or unidentified person, **www.missingpeople.org.uk**

National Society for the Prevention of Cruelty to Children (NSPCC), Weston House, 42 Curtain Road, London EC2A 3NH, tel 020 7825 2500; in Wales, 13th Floor, Capital Tower, Greyfriars Road, Cardiff, CF10 3AG; tel, 029 2026 7000, also Regional Offices in the UK, runs a free 24hr child protection helpline for children, young people & parents tel 0808 800 5000, **www.nspcc.org.uk**.

NORCAP, 112 Church Road, Wheatley, Oxfordshire OX33 1LU, tel 01865 875 000, provides advice & support for adopted people & their birth relatives who wish to get in touch. Open Mon-Wed, 10.00am-1.00pm, 1.30pm-4.30pm, Thu, 12noon-4.30pm, Fri, 10.00am-4.00pm, **www.norcap.org.uk**.

One-Parent Families/Gingerbread, 255 Kentish Town Road, London NW5 2LX, tel 020 7428 5400, provides free information for lone parents on many subjects including benefits, legal rights, childcare & divorce. A lone-parent helpline is open Mon, Tue, Thu, Fri 9.00am-5.00pm, Wed 9.00am-8.00pm, tel 0800 018 5026, **www.oneparentfamilies.org.uk**.

Parentline Plus, 520 Highgate Studios, 53-79 Highgate Road, Kentish Town, London, NW5 1TL, 020 7284 5500, acts mainly as a service for parents, but will also provide information & support for families. Free 24hr helpline, tel 0808 800 2222, **www.parentlineplus.org.uk**.

Rights of Women, 52-54 Featherstone Street, London EC1Y 8RT, tel, 020 7251 6575/6, provides free advice to women on their legal rights, including family law, domestic & sexual violence & discrimination. A legal advice line, tel 020 7251 6577, is open Tue, Wed, Thurs, 2.00pm-4.00pm & 7.00pm-9.00pm, & Fri 12noon-2.00pm. A sexual violence legal advice line, tel 020 7251 8887 is open Mon 11.00am-1.00pm, & Tue 10.00am-12noon, **www.rightsofwomen.org.uk**

Runaway provides a free helpline, tel 0808 800 70 70, for young people who have run away or been forced to leave home or care, **www.missingpeople.org.uk**.

Women's Aid, PO Box 391, Bristol BS99 7WS, tel 0117 944 44 11; in Wales, Welsh Women's Aid, 38-48 Crwys Road, Cardiff, CF24 4NN, tel, 029 2039 9874, gives information, support & advice for women experiencing domestic violence in the home. 24-hour helpline in England, tel 0808 20 00 247, **www.womensaid.org.uk**; in Wales, tel 0808 80 10 800. The website, **www.thehideout.org.uk** provides practical help for young people who are witnessing or experiencing domestic violence.

Home

The Advisory Service for Squatters, Angel Alley, 84b Whitechapel High Street, London E1 7QX, tel 020 3216 0099 (or 0845 644 5814 for land lines outside London), is a volunteer organisation offering a daily advice service for squatters and homeless people, **www.squatter.org.uk**.

Centrepoint, Central House, 25 Camperdown Street, London E1 8DZ,tel, 0845 466 3400, 9.00am-5.30pm, Mon-Fri: provides a range of services including emergency night shelters & short stay hostels. The website, **www.centrepoint.org.uk**, gives a great deal of help & advice on finding emergency accommodation.

The Foyer Federation, 3rd Floor, 5-9 Hatton Wall, London EC1N 8HX, tel 020 7430 2212, a UK-wide youth homeless charity providing accommodation, education & training opportunities for young people with housing needs. For details of your nearest Foyer see **www.foyer.net**.

Shelter, 88 Old Street, London EC1V 9HU, tel 0845 458 4590; in Wales, 25 Walter Road, Swansea, SA1 5NN, tel, 01792 469400, campaigns to improve the housing conditions & rights of private tenants. Shelter has a network of housing aid centres across the country (details from the website or phone numbers above) & runs Shelter helpline, a free 24hr national housing helpline tel 0808 800 4444; in Wales also 0845 075 5005, **www.shelter.org.uk**, **www.sheltercymru.org.uk**

Leisure

CitizenCard, 36 Bromells Road, London, SW4 0BG, can provide a photo-ID card & proof of age. Application forms are available from the website, the address above, supermarkets, post offices, off-licences or newsagents, **www.citizencard.com**.

Countryside Access, for information on access to land in England, see **www.countrysideaccess.gov.uk**, for Wales, see the Countryside Council for Wales, **www.ccw.gov.uk**.

Environment Agency has offices around the country. For general enquiries tel 08708 506 506 or see www.environment-agency.gov.uk. For information about flooding in your area, contact the Floodline, tel 0845 988 1188. A free 24hr emergency phone line can be used to report any environmental incident, tel 0800 80 70 60.

Royal Society for the Prevention of Cruelty to Animals (RSPCA), have a 24hr emergency cruelty & advice line for people who wish to report an animal in distress, tel 0300 1234 999. For other information contact The RSPCA Enquiries Service, Wilberforce Way, Southwater, Horsham, West Sussex RH13 9RS, tel 0300 1234 555, (9.00am-5.00pm, Mon-Fri), **www.rspca.org.uk**.

Royal Society for Protection of Birds (RSPB), UK HQ, The Lodge, Potton Road, Sandy, Bedfordshire, SG19 2DL, tel, 01767 680551, in Wales, Sutherland House, Castlebridge, Cowbridge Road East, Cardiff, CF11 9AB, tel, 02920 353000, for advice on protected birds, **www.rspb.org.uk**.

Travel and transport

ABTA (The Association of British Travel Agents), 68-71 Newman Street, London W1T 3AH, for information & advice over problems with package holidays, tel 020 7637 2444, Mon-Fri, 9.00am-5.30pm, **www.abta.com**.

Department of Transport, for information on motoring & transport law, see website, write to The Enquiry Service, Dept for Transport, Great Minster House, 76 Marsham Street, London SW1P 4DR, or tel 020 7944 8300 (8.30am-5.30pm, Mon-Fri), **www.dft.gov.uk**,

Driving Standards Agency, The Axis Building, 112 Upper Parliament Street, Nottingham, NG1 6LP, tel, 0115 936 6666 for information on driving tests for cars & compulsory basic training for motorcyclists. To book a theory test, tel 0300 200 1122 (Welsh speakers, tel 0300 2001133), Mon-Fri, 8.00am-6.00pm, write to DSA Customer Services, PO Box 381, Salford, M50 3UW, or book online at the DSA website. For a practical test, telephone the same numbers as for the theory tests above, write to DSA, PO Box 280, Newcastle-upon-Tyne, NE 99 1FP, book on line, or obtain a booking form from your driving school, or local test centre, **www.dsa.gov.uk**.

DVLA, (Driver & Vehicle Licensing Agency) Swansea SA6 7JL, for enquiries about driving licences, tax discs or the registration details of a particular vehicle. Driver enquiries, tel 0870 240 0009 or write to the Driver Customer Services at the address above; vehicle enquiries, tel 0870 240 0010 or write to the Vehicle Customer Services at the address above, but use the postcode SA99 1AR. Both lines are open Mon-Fri, 8.00am-8.30pm, Sat, 8.00am-5.30pm, **www.dvla.gov.uk**.

Euro<26 Card, a card for those aged between 12 & 25, providing discount in over 100,000 outlets in more than 41 countries, including cinemas, concerts, festivals, and travel, costing £7 for one year or £10 for two years. To order, write to, phone, or call Euro 26 Applications, Gateshead Youth Council, 12 Gladstone Terrace, Gateshead, Tyne & Wear, NE8 4DY, tel 0191 490 1900. In Wales Canllaw Online, EURO<26, Caerphilly Business Park, Van Court, Van Road, Caerphilly, CF83 3ED, tel, 029 2088 7868, or apply on line at **www.nya.org.uk/euro26**.

HM Revenue & Customs, for free information leaflets for travellers, see **www.hmrc.gov.uk**, and click on travel information.

Identity & Passport Service (IPS) There are five regional offices in England & Wales (London, Durham, Liverpool, Peterborough & Newport). Contact details are given on the website & on passport application forms, available from the Post Office. For information on applying for a passport, fees, notice required etc, see **www.ips.gov.uk** or call the 24-hour Passport Adviceline 0300 222 0000.

National Express Group plc, 7 Triton Square, London NW1 3HG, tel, 08450 130 130 for information on coach rail & local bus travel & cheap tickets for people aged 16-26 & those in full-time education. For bus travel enquiries, call 0871 200 2233; for rail travel enquiries call 08457 48 49 50, **www.nationalexpress.com**. For the disabled persons travel helpline, tel 08717 818179.

Royal Society for the Prevention of Accidents (RoSPA), Edgbaston Park, 353 Bristol Road, Birmingham B5 7ST, tel 0121 248 2000. In Wales, 2nd Floor,2 Cwrt-y-Park, Park Ty Glas, Cardiff Business Park, Llanishen, Cardiff, CF14 5GH, tel, 02920 250600, for information on all aspects of safety, and the prevention of accidents at work in the home, on the roads, in schools etc, **www.rospa.com**.

ValidateUK, Main House, Bishop's Yard, Corbridge, Northumberland NE45 5LA, tel 01434 634996, open Mon-Fri, 9.00am-5.00pm, operates a national, approved proof of age scheme. Cards cost £10. Application forms available by phone, post, or downloadable from **www.validateuk.co.uk**.

Young Persons Railcard, available to 16-25 year olds (& 26+ in full-time education) costing £24 pa (£65 for 3 years), providing a one-third discount on many UK rail journeys, & some bus & boat links. Apply at a staffed station, or rail-appointed travel agent, taking a passport-sized photograph & proof of age. Application forms downloadable from website, **www.youngpersons-railcard.co.uk**.

Police and courts

Citizens Advice Bureaux have trained staff who can give free legal advice & suggest solicitors able to deal with your particular problem. See General section, for details.

Community Legal Advice, provides free information on legal services to those eligible for legal aid (eg on low income &/or benefits), tel 0845 345 4 345, Mon-Fri, 9.00am-6.30pm, **www.clsdirect.org.uk**.

The Court Service, HMCS Headquarters, Customer Service Unit, 4th Floor, 102 Petty France, London SW1H 9AJ publishes the Courts' Charter explaining how the court system works & what you can expect if you go to court as a defendant, plaintiff, witness or member of a jury - available from your local court or Citizens Advice Bureau, **www.hmcourts-service.gov.uk**.

The Criminal Justice System online provides information about the criminal justice system in England & Wales for victims, witnesses, jurors, or those accused or convicted of a crime, **www.cjsonline.gov.uk**

Independent Police Complaints Commission (IPCC), 90 High Holborn, London WC1V 6BH; in Wales, Eastern Business Park, Wern Fawr Lane, St Mellons, Cardiff, CF3 5EA, is the official body overseeing complaints against the police. For information on how to make a complaint if you have witnessed or believe you have suffered police misconduct, tel 08453 002 002, (press 1 at prompt), Mon-Fri, 9.00am-5.00pm, **www.ipcc.gov.uk**

Law, government and human rights

POLITICAL PARTIES

Conservative Party, 30 Millbank, London, SW1P 4DP, tel 020 7222 9000, **www.conservatives.com**; in Wales, 4 Pennline Road, Whitchurch, Cardiff, CF14 2XS, tel, 029 2061 6031, **www.conservatives.com/wales**.

Green Party, 1a Waterlow Road, London N19 5NJ, tel 020 7272 4474, www.greenparty.org.uk; in Wales, 40 Ewenny Road, Bridgend, CF31 3HR, tel, 0845 458 1026, **www.walesgreenparty.org.uk**.

Labour Party, 39 Victoria Street, London SW1H 0HA, tel 08705 900 200; address for correspondence, Eldon House, Regent Centre, Newcastle-upon-Tyne, NE3 3PW, **www.labour.org.uk**; in Wales, Transport House, 1 Cathedral Road, Cardiff, CF11 9HA, tel, 029 2087 7700, **www.welshlabour.org.uk**.

Liberal Democrats, 4 Cowley St., London SW1P 3NB, tel 020 7222 7999, www.libdems.org.uk; in Wales Ground Floor, Blake Court, Schooner Way, Butetown, Cardiff, CF10 4DW, tel, 029 2031 3400, **www.welshlibdems.org.uk**.

Plaid Cymru, the Party of Wales, Ty Gwynfor, Marine Chambers, Anson Court, Atlantic Wharf, Cardiff, CF10 4AL, tel, 029 2047 2272, **www.plaidcymru.org**

GENERAL

Ministry of Justice, 102 Petty France, London, SW1H 9AJ,tel, 020 3334 3555, has responsibility, amongst other things, for the administration of the Human Rights Act and produces a number of free guides to the Act, tel 020 3334 3734, or see **http://www.justice.gov.uk/**what we do/humanrights.htm See also the Human Rights pages of **www.direct.gov.uk**

House of Commons Information Office, House of Commons, Norman Shaw North, London SW1A 2TT, tel 020 7219 4272, a public information service on the working & proceedings of Parliament, **www.parliament.uk**. A similar information service is offered by the House of Lords Information Office, House of Lords, London SW1A 0PW, tel, 020 7219 3107.

The Information Commissioner's Office, Wycliffe House, Water Lane, Wilmslow, Cheshire, SK9 5AF, tel, 01625 54 57 45; for Wales, Cambrian Buildings, Mount Stuart Square, Cardiff, CF10 5FL, tel, 029 2044 8044, has responsibility for overseeing the workings of the Data Protection & Freedom of Information Acts. A helpline is open during normal office hours, tel 08456 30 60 60, **www.ico.gov.uk**

The European Union

The Council of Europe works to find solutions to some of the problems facing European society, Avenue de L'Europe, 67075 Strasbourg Cedex, France, tel +33(0)3 88 41 20 33, **www.coe.int**.

European Commission, for your nearest centre for information, tel 020 7973 1992. UK offices, 8 Storey's Gate, London, SW1P 3AT & 2 Caspian Point, Caspian Way, Cardiff, CF10 4QQ, tel, 029 2089 5020, **www.europe.org.uk**

European Parliament Information Office, 2 Queen Anne's Gate, London SW1H 9AA, tel, 020 7227 4300, **www.europarl.org.uk**, provides information about the European Parliament, its structures & activities, the European Commission & information about the political groups in the Parliament, including your local MEPs.

Europe Direct is a European-wide service which can answer questions about the European Union. A freephone information service is open 8.00am-5.30pm, tel 00800 67891011, where you can speak in your own language, **http://ec.europa.eu/europedirect**.

European Youth Forum (EYF), Rue Joseph II straat 120, B-1000 Brussels, tel, +32 2 230 64 90 represents youth organisations from all over Europe, channelling information & opinions between young people & decision-makers, **www.youthforum.org**.

Organising Bureau of School Students Unions, Rue de la Sablonniere 20, 1000 Brussels, Belgium, tel +32(0) 264 72 390. OBESSU coordinates national organisations of school students, **www.obessu.org**.